LEXICAL AIDS FOR STUDENTS OF NEW TESTAMENT GREEK

BRUCE M. METZGER

George L. Collord Professor of
New Testament Language and Literature
Princeton Theological Seminary

NEW EDITION

BASIL BLACKWELL

OXFORD

1980

TYPE COMPOSED IN GREAT BRITAIN
AT THE UNIVERSITY PRESS, OXFORD
PRINTED BY BILLING AND SONS LTD
GUILDFORD, LONDON AND WORCESTER

Library

Harcourt Hill

Library

WITHDRAWN

REFERENCE ONLY

OXFORD
BROOKES
UNIVERSITY   Directorate of **Learning Resources**

ALSO BY BRUCE M. METZGER

οὐ πόλλ' ἀλλὰ πολύ   'not quantity but quality'

(*literally*, 'not many things but much')

μελέτη τὸ πᾶν   'practice makes perfect'

(*literally*, 'practice [is] everything')

PREFACE

ACCORDING to the psychologist, man learns by associating the new with the old, the strange with the familiar. In studying a foreign language, therefore, the beginner will do well to observe whatever similarities may exist between his own and the other language.

Part I of the following *Lexical Aids* makes use of this principle of associative learning by supplying, after the English definitions of Greek words, such English derivatives as may be of assistance in remembering the meaning of the Greek vocabulary. The Greek words in the list, furthermore, have been selected and arranged in accord with their frequency of occurrence in the New Testament.

Part II makes a different application of the same psychological principle. Here are exhibited the family relationships among words of frequent and less frequent occurrence. After a student has become acquainted with a minimum working vocabulary of words that occur many times in the New Testament he can make more rapid progress in acquiring a larger vocabulary by learning such additional words as resemble in general meaning and form those which he already knows.

What proportion of attention should be devoted to Part I ('Words Classified According to Their Frequency') before beginning to employ at the same time Part II ('Words Classified According to Their Root') can be determined on the basis of economy of time and effort. A judicious and faithful use of both Parts will speed the day when the beginner can read the Greek Testament with pleasure and profit.

October 1, 1946

PREFACE TO THE BRITISH EDITION

WHEN this little booklet was first issued in 1946 no one—and least of all the compiler—could have foreseen that some thirty years later it would exist in more than one hundred and thirty thousand copies and in translations into Malagasy (1967) and Korean (1968). That Basil Blackwell are now issuing a British edition, which will bring it into still wider circulation, is naturally of no little satisfaction to me. Except for several minor typographical corrections, the text of the present printing is that of the 'New Edition' issued in 1969. For this reason the list of Greek lexicons on pp. 5–6 makes no reference to the second edition of Bauer-Arndt-Gingrich's *Greek–English Lexicon*, issued in 1979.

It may be confessed here that the Greek colophon which stands on the last page is doubly appropriate—no less for the compiler than for the user of this booklet. This couplet, with which many a weary scribe in the Byzantine period brought his work of copying a manuscript to a close, may be rendered, 'As travellers rejoice to see their native land, so also is the end of a book to those who labour!'

BRUCE M. METZGER

July 23, 1980

CONTENTS

WORDS CLASSIFIED ACCORDING TO THEIR FREQUENCY

ACCORDING to statistics collected by Robert Morgenthaler,[1] the Greek New Testament makes use of 5,436 different Greek words. More than one half of these (namely, 3,246 words) occur only once, twice, or thrice in the entire New Testament. Of the remainder, about eleven hundred occur ten or more times. All of these, with the exception of proper names,[2] are included in the following word lists (comprising a total of 1,067 words), and are arranged in descending order of their frequency.

The usefulness of such lists is obvious. By consulting them the beginner will not, so to speak, waste his time memorizing words that occur only rarely in the New Testament. He can be assured that when he has learned, say, the first 513 words in the lists he then knows *all* of the words (other than the proper names) that occur at least 25 times in the New Testament.

The beginner of any foreign language always finds it easier to acquire a working knowledge of the vocabulary if he is shown parallels between it and his own language. Although several grammars for beginners of Classical Greek are provided with such mnemonic aids (as, for example, the grammars by H. L. Crosby and J. N. Schaeffer, and by A. S. Way), grammarians of New Testament Greek have been slow in adopting this pedagogically sound procedure. As a start in this direction there have been added to the following frequency word lists such English derivatives as seemed likely to prove helpful to the student

[1] *Statistik des neutestamentlichen Wortschatzes* (Zurich, 1958). The statistics are based on the 21st edition of the Nestle Greek New Testament. According to Morgenthaler (p. 26), the total number of words in the entire Greek New Testament is 137,490 words. Every seventh word is a definite article, every fifteenth word an 'and,' and every twenty-fifth word an αὐτός. The ten most frequently used words comprise about 45,000 of the total 137,328 words, and the approximately 170 words that occur more than one hundred times each comprise about 100,000 words of the total text (that is, about five-sevenths of the New Testament).

[2] As a rule the proper names in the Greek New Testament so closely resemble the corresponding names in English as to occasion very little difficulty of recognition. A table of equivalent letters is given below on p. 3.

of New Testament Greek. It need scarcely be mentioned that not every Greek word has an English derivative. Nevertheless, a surprisingly large proportion of the following words can be supplied with more or less well-known English derivatives.[1] The derivative, which is italicized and enclosed within parentheses, is not to be confused with the definition of the Greek word. The definition is to be memorized; the derivative is intended to be of assistance in remembering the definition. Although many other examples of English derivations from these Greek words might have been cited, those which are given were chosen with an eye to the probable interests of the type of student who will make use of this booklet. That is, whenever it was possible to do so, derivatives were provided that involve theological, ecclesiastical, or patristic terminology.

In some instances the derivative is not direct but is from a closely related word in Greek. In these cases the English word is introduced by the abbreviation 'cf.' (= 'compare'). Thus, for example, the definition of the noun διδάσκαλος is followed by '(cf. *didactic*),' for, although no noun in English is a direct derivative of διδάσκαλος, the adjective *didactic*, being derived from a closely related Greek word (διδακτικός), will serve as a mnemonic aid in remembering the meaning of διδάσκαλος. In a few instances, when not even this sort of indirect derivative is available in English, a cognate word is cited. Thus, after the definition of πατήρ one finds '(akin to *paternal*),' for *paternal* closely resembles πατήρ because the English word is derived from the Latin *pater*, which in turn is a cognate of the Greek word.[2]

Attention may be called to the occasional use of a word or phrase enclosed within parentheses in conjunction with the definition of a Greek word. Thus, ἀποστέλλω is defined '*I send* (with a commission)'. The words within parentheses will not be confused with the English derivative, for the latter is in every case printed in italics. Again, it will be observed that a semi-colon is used (1) to separate quite diverse English definitions of the same Greek word, and (2) to separate two or more English derivatives from one another.

The following table of equivalent letters and diphthongs will be of assistance in learning to become aware of many English derivatives

---

[1] To be exact, 467 of the 1066 words that occur ten times or more are provided with English derivatives. This is about 45 per cent.

[2] For further information regarding cognate words, see Appendix I.

other than those which are cited by way of example. The Greek
letters whose transliteration is immediately obvious are not included.

CONSONANTS

Greek	English	Examples
γγ	*ng*	εὐαγγέλιον, *evangel*
ζ	*z*	ζωή, *Zoe*
κ	*c* (sometimes *k*)[1]	ἐκκλησία, *ecclesiastic* κινέω, *kinetic* εἰκών, *icon* (also *ikon*)
ξ	*x*	ξύλον, *xylo*phone
φ	*ph*	φωνή, *-phone*
χ	*ch*	εὐχαριστία, *Eucharist*
ψ	*ps*	ψεύδομαι, *pseudo-*

VOWELS AND DIPHTHONGS

Greek	English	Examples
η	*e*	ζωή, *Zoe*
(initial) ι (followed by a vowel)	*j*	ἰῶτα, *jot* 'Ιησοῦς, *Jesus*
υ	*y*	ψυχή, *psyche*
αι	*e* (or *ae*)	αἷμα, *hemo*globin (or *haemo-*)
ει	*i* (or *ei*)	εἰκών, *icon* δείκνυμι, *deictic*
ευ	*eu*, before a vowel *ev*	εὐ+φημί, *euphemism* εὐαγγέλιον, *evangel*
οι	*e* (or *oe*)	οἰκουμενικός, *ecumenical* (also *oecumenical*)
ου	*u*	οὐ+τόπος, *Utopia*
(final) ια	*y*	εὐλογία, *eulogy*

A few observations concerning the most efficient ways in which to
use the following word lists will not be out of place. The usual and
time-tested procedure is to concentrate on a Greek word and to repeat
it to oneself over and over again with the English definition. In doing
so one should be careful always to put the stress on the syllable of the

---

[1] In general when a Greek word has entered English through Latin it has *c* for
kappa; when it has come direct, it has *k*.

Greek word which carries the accent mark. Otherwise, if, for instance, ἀδελφός be pronounced *a'del-fos* today, and *a-del'fos* tomorrow, and *a-del-fos'* at another time, the labor of learning the one Greek word is practically tripled.

Of great importance in the proper pronunciation of Greek words is a knowledge of the rules governing their division into syllables. These principles are simple. There are as many syllables in a Greek word as separate vowels or diphthongs. (1) A single consonant standing between two vowels in one word belongs with the second vowel, as ἀ-γά-πη. (2) A group of consonants that can begin a word (such combinations may be seen in a lexicon), and a group formed by a consonant followed by μ or ν, belongs with the second vowel. (3) A group of consonants that cannot begin a word is divided between two syllables, as ἐλ-πίς, ἀ-μαρ-τά-νω. Doubled consonants are divided, as θά-λασ-σα. (4) Compound words divide at the point of union, as εἰσ-φέρω, συν-έχω.

An exceedingly helpful method of learning a foreign language is to write the unfamiliar words. Indeed, according to the author of a popular treatise on the study of languages, this method ought to be practiced by every one learning a new language. Frederick Bodmer declares, 'Pen (or pencil) and paper are essential help. We are most apt to forget what we take in by ear, least likely to forget what we learn by touch. No one who has learned to swim or cycle forgets the trick of doing so.'[1] Most students discover that the effort of writing helps to fix their attention on the task at hand and thus impresses the new words more firmly in their memory. It is recommended that, in order to gain the greatest benefit from the following word lists, the student utilize both the oral and the written disciplines. Moreover, in addition to memorizing lists of words, the highest degree of proficiency in translating the New Testament can be attained only if long sections of the Greek text are read, preferably aloud.

In counting the frequency of Greek words in the New Testament, the author utilized W. F. Moulton and A. S. Geden's *Concordance to the Greek Testament*, 2nd edn. (Edinburgh, 1899). It may be mentioned that Moulton and Geden's orthography follows that of Westcott and Hort in their edition of the Greek New Testament.

[1] *The Loom of Language* (New York, 1944), p. 28.

The definitions have been purposely kept brief and pointed, yet it is hoped that no denotation which occurs with any degree of frequency has been neglected. For further information concerning various connotations and nuances of meaning, the following standard lexicons may be consulted.

SELECTED BIBLIOGRAPHY OF GREEK LEXICONS

ABBOTT-SMITH, G., *A Manual Greek Lexicon of the New Testament* (3rd edn., Edinburgh, 1937).

Reasonably complete and not unwieldy, but does not make full use of new material.

ARNDT, WILLIAM F., and GINGRICH, F. WILBUR, *A Greek–English Lexicon of the New Testament and other early Christian Literature*, a translation and adaptation of Walter Bauer's *Griechisch-Deutsches Wörterbuch zu den Schriften des Neuen Testament usw.*, 4te Aufl., Berlin, 1949–52 (Chicago and Cambridge, 1957).

Best of New Testament lexicons, with rich bibliographical data. The 5th edition of Bauer's Greek–German lexicon was published in 1958.

GINGRICH, F. WILBUR, *Shorter Lexicon of the Greek New Testament* (Chicago and London, 1965).

A condensation of the Bauer–Arndt–Gingrich lexicon, without bibliographical data.

KITTEL, GERHARD (ed.), *Theologisches Wörterbuch zum Neuen Testament*, 9 vols. (Stuttgart, 1933–); English trans. by Geoffrey W. Bromiley, *Theological Dictionary of the New Testament* (Grand Rapids, 1964–).

Combines strict philological method with theological insight; an unparalleled source of information. Vols. 5 ff. are edited by Gerhard Friedrich.

LAMPE, G. W. H.,(ed.), *A Patristic Greek Lexicon*, fascicles 1–5 (Oxford, 1961–8).

The authoritative work in its field. Useful in tracing the early history of the exegesis of New Testament words and passages.

LIDDELL, H. G., and SCOTT, R., *A Greek–English Lexicon*, new edn., revised and augmented throughout by H. S. Jones, assisted by R. McKenzie (Oxford, 1925–40).

The standard lexicon of Classical Greek. A *Supplement*, edited by E. A. Barber, with the assistance of P. Maas, M. Scheller, and M. L. West (Oxford, 1968), incorporates addenda and corrigenda.

5

MOULTON, J. H., and MILLIGAN, G., *The Vocabulary of the Greek Testament Illustrated from the Papyri and Other Non-Literary Sources* (London, 1914–29; one vol. edn., 1930).

Defines only those words on which the editors found fresh information in the papyri and other non-literary sources; unsurpassed in its field.

NEWMAN, BARCLAY M., Jr., *A Concise Greek–English Dictionary of the New Testament* (New York, 1971).

A companion volume to the United Bible Societies' edition of the Greek New Testament.

PREISIGKE, FRIEDRICH, *Wörterbuch der griechischen Papyrusurkunden mit Einschluß der griechischen Inschriften, Aufschriften, Ostraka, Mumienschilder, usw., aus Ägypten*, 3 vols. (Berlin, 1925–31).

A general lexicon of the Greek papyri. A new edition is appearing as vols. 4 ff. (1944–).

PRING, J. T., *The Oxford Dictionary of Modern Greek (Greek–English)* (Oxford, 1965).

SOUTER, ALEXANDER, *A Pocket Lexicon to the Greek New Testament* (Oxford, 1916).

Fresh, vivid definitions; its faults are those of extreme brevity and lack of helps for locating forms.

ZORELL, FRANCISCUS, *Lexicon Graecum Novi Testamenti*, 3rd edn. (Paris, 1961).

A useful Greek to Latin lexicon by a capable Jesuit scholar.

FREQUENCY WORD LISTS

Words occurring:			Words occurring:		
more than 500 times,	pp.	7–8	25 times,	pp.	23–24
201 to 500 times,	pp.	8–10	24 times,		p. 24
151 to 200 times,	pp.	10–11	23 times,	pp.	24–25
121 to 150 times,	pp.	11–12	22 times,		p. 25
101 to 120 times,	pp.	12–13	21 times,	pp.	25–26
91 to 100 times,		p. 13	20 times,		p. 26
81 to 90 times,	pp.	13–14	19 times,		p. 27
71 to 80 times,	pp.	14–15	18 times,	pp.	27–28
61 to 70 times,		p. 15	17 times,	pp.	28–29
56 to 60 times,		p. 16	16 times,	pp.	29–30
50 to 55 times,	pp.	16–17	15 times,	pp.	30–32
46 to 49 times,	pp.	17–18	14 times,	pp.	32–33
42 to 45 times,		p. 18	13 times,	pp.	33–34
38 to 41 times,	pp.	18–19	12 times,	pp.	34–36
34 to 37 times,	pp.	19–20	11 times,	pp.	36–38
32 or 33 times,	pp.	20–21	10 times,	pp.	38–40
30 or 31 times,	pp.	21–22			
28 or 29 times,		p. 22			
26 or 27 times,	pp.	22–23			

WORDS OCCURRING MORE THAN 500 TIMES

ἄνθρωπος, -ου, ὁ, *a man* (*anthropo*logy)

ἀπό, with the gen., *from* (*apo*stasy, standing [στῆναι] off from)

αὐτός, -ή, -ό, *himself, herself, itself, same*; *he, she, it* (*auto*soterism, the doctrine that man is saved by his own efforts or character)

γάρ, *for*

γίνομαι, *I become, am*

δέ, *but, and*

διά, with the gen., *through*; with the acc., *on account of* (*dia*meter, measure across or through)

ἐγώ, *I* (*ego*tism)

εἰμί, *I am*

εἶπον, *I said* (cf. *epic*)

εἰς, with the acc., *into* (*eis*egesis, faulty interpretation of a text by read-
ing into it one's own ideas)

ἐκ, ἐξ, with the gen., *out of, from* (*ec*stasy, state of being [literally,
standing, στῆναι] out of one's senses; *ex*odus, a going [literally, a way,
ὁδός] out)

ἐν, with the dat., *in* (*en*thusiast, one possessed or inspired by a god
[ἔνθεος])

ἐπί, with the gen., *over, on, at the time of*; with the dat., *on the basis of, at*;
with the acc., *on, to, against* (*epi*dermis, upon the skin [δέρμα])

ἔρχομαι, *I come, go*

ἔχω, *I have, hold*

θεός, -οῦ, ὁ, *a god, God* (*theo*logy)

ἵνα, *in order that, that*

καί, *and, even, also*

κατά, with the gen., *down from, against*; with the acc., *according to,
throughout, during* (*cata*clysm, a washing down or against)

κύριος, -ov, ὁ, *a lord, the Lord*

λέγω, *I say, speak* (all words ending in -*ologue* or -*ology*)

μή, *not, lest*

ὁ, ἡ, τό, *the*

ὅς, ἥ, ὅ, *who, which*

ὅτι, *that, because*

οὗτος, αὕτη, τοῦτο, *this*; *he, her, it*

οὐ, οὐκ, οὐχ, *not* (*u*topia, no place [τόπος])

πᾶς, πᾶσα, πᾶν, *every, all* (*Pan*-American)

ποιέω, *I do, make* (*poem*; pharmaco*poeia*, making of drugs)

πρός, with the acc., *to, towards, with* (*pros*elyte, one who has come [root
of ἐλθεῖν] to another religion)

σύ, *thou*

τίς, τί, *who? what? which? why?*

τις, τι *someone, something, a certain one, a certain thing, anyone, anything*

ὡς, *as, that, how, about*

WORDS OCCURRING 201 TO 500 TIMES

ἅγιος, -α, -ον, *holy*; plural as a noun, *saints* (*Hagio*grapha, books of the
Hebrew Scriptures not included under Law and Prophets)

ἀδελφός, -οῦ, ὁ, *brother* (Phil*adelphia*, [city of] brotherly love [φιλία])

ἀκούω, *I hear* (*acoustics*)

8

ἀλλά, *but, except*

ἀνήρ, ἀνδρός, ὁ, *a man* (polyandry, having many husbands)

ἀποκρίνομαι, *I answer*

γῆ, γῆς, ἡ, *the earth* (geopolitics)

γινώσκω, *I come to know, learn, know, realize*

γυνή, γυναικός, ἡ, *a woman, wife* (misogynist, a woman-hater [μισέω])

δίδωμι, *I give* (antidote)

δύναμαι, *I am powerful, able* (cf. dynamite)

ἐάν, *if*

ἑαυτοῦ, *of himself*

εἰ, *if*

εἶδον, *I saw* (idea)

εἷς, μία, ἕν, *one* (henotheism, belief in one God without asserting that he is the only God)

ἐκεῖνος, -η, -ο, *that*

ἐξέρχομαι, *I go out*

ἤ, *or*

ἡμέρα, -ας, ἡ, *a day* (ephemeral, for [ἐφ' (= ἐπί)] a day)

θέλω, *I will, wish, desire* (Monothelite, one who holds that Christ has but one will, the divine; condemned by the Sixth General Council, A.D. 680)

λαλέω, *I speak* (cf. glossolalia, the gift of speaking in tongues [1 Cor. 14])

λαμβάνω, *I take, receive* (epilepsy, a taking or seizing upon)

λόγος, -ου, ὁ, *a word, the Word* (logic)

μαθητής, -οῦ, ὁ, *a disciple*

μετά, with the gen., *with*; with the acc., *after* (metaphysics, beyond or after [Aristotle's treatise on] physics)

οἶδα, *I know*

ὄνομα, -ατος, τό, *a name* (onomatopoeia, making [ποιεῖν] a name or word [in imitation of natural sounds], as 'buzz')

οὐδείς, οὐδεμία, οὐδέν, *no one, none, nothing, no*

οὖν, *therefore, then, accordingly*

οὐρανός, -οῦ, ὁ, *heaven* (the planet Uranus; the element uranium)

οὕτως, *thus*

πατήρ, πατρός, ὁ, *father* (akin to paternal)

περί, with the gen., *concerning, about*; with the acc., *around* (perimeter, measure around)

πιστεύω, *I have faith (in), believe*

πίστις, -εως, ἡ, *faith, belief, trust*

9

πνεῦμα, -ατος, τό, a spirit, the Spirit (pneumatology, the doctrine of the Holy Spirit)

πολύς, πολλή, πολύ, much; plural, many (polytheism)

υἱός, -οῦ, ὁ, a son

ὑπό, with the gen., by; with the acc., under (hypodermic, under the skin [δέρμα])

WORDS OCCURRING 151 TO 200 TIMES

ἄγγελος, -ου, ὁ, a messenger, an angel (angel)

ἁμαρτία, -ας, ἡ, a sin, sin (hamartiology, the doctrine of sin)

ἄν, an untranslatable word, the effect of which is to make a statement contingent which would otherwise be definite

βασιλεία, -ας, ἡ, a kingdom

γράφω, I write (palaeography, the study of ancient [παλαιός] writing)

δόξα, -ης, ἡ, glory (doxology)

ἔθνος, -ους, τό, a nation; plural, the Gentiles (ethnology)

εἰσέρχομαι, I go or come in or into, enter

ἔργον, -ου, τό, work (energy)

ἐσθίω, I eat (akin to edible)

εὑρίσκω, I find (heuristic, the method in education by which a pupil is set to find out things for himself; eureka, 'I have found [it]!'— Archimedes

ἰδού, see! behold!

ἵστημι, I cause to stand, I stand (akin to stand)

καθώς, as, even as

καρδία, -ας, ἡ, the heart (cardiac)

κόσμος, ου, ὁ, the world (cosmic, cosmos)

μέγας, μεγάλη, μέγα, large, great (megaphone; omega [literally, great 'o'])

μέν, postpositive particle, on the one hand, indeed (often it is better left untranslated and its presence shown by stress of the voice and by translating a following δέ by 'but')

νεκρός, -ά, -όν, dead; as a noun, a dead body, a corpse (necropolis, city of the dead, a cemetery)

νόμος, -ου, ὁ, a law, the Law (Deuteronomy, the second [statement of the] law)

ὅστις, ἥτις, ὅτι, whoever, whichever, whatever

ὄχλος, -ου, ὁ, a crowd, multitude (ochlocracy, mob-rule)

παρά, with the gen. from; with the dat., beside, in the presence of; with

the acc., *alongside of* (*para*graph, originally, in manuscripts, a stroke
or line drawn in the margin *beside* the column of writing to mark
the division of sections)

πόλις, -εως, ἡ, *a city* (Nea*polis*, 'New City,' Acts 16: 11; Constan-
tino*ple*, Constantine's City)

πορεύομαι, *I go, proceed*

τε, (an enclitic connective particle, weaker in force than καί), *and*

τότε, *then, at that time*

ὑπέρ, with the gen., *in behalf of*; with the acc., *above* (*hyper*critical)

χάρις, -ιτος, ἡ, *grace* (*Charissa*, [girl's name])

χείρ, χειρός, ἡ, *a hand* (*chiro*graphy, handwriting)

WORDS OCCURRING 121 TO 150 TIMES

ἀγαπάω, *I love*

αἰών, -ῶνος, ὁ, *an age* (*aeon*)

ἄλλος, -η, -ο, *other, another* (*all*egory, description of one thing under the
image of another)

ἀμήν, *verily, truly, amen* (*amen*)

ἀποστέλλω, *I send* (with a commission) (cf. *Apostle*)

ἀρχιερεύς, -έως, ὁ, *chief priest, high priest*

ἀφίημι, *I let go, permit, forgive* (*aphesis*, the gradual loss of a short unaccented initial vowel, as 'squire' for 'esquire')

βάλλω, *I throw, put* (*ballistics*, the science of the motion of projectiles)

βλέπω, *I see*

δοῦλος, -ου, ὁ, *a slave*

δύο, *two* (*dyad*)

ἐγείρω, *I raise up*

ἕως, *until*; with the gen., *as far as*

ζάω, *I live*

ζωή, -ῆς, ἡ, *life* (*Zoe* [girl's name])

καλέω, *I call, name, invite*

λαός, -οῦ, ὁ, *a people* (*laity*)

νῦν, *now*

ὅταν, *whenever*

οὐδέ, *and not, not even, neither, nor*

πάλιν, *again* (*palim*psest, a manuscript which has been used again, the
earlier writing having been erased [ψῆν, to scrape or erase])

παραδίδωμι, *I hand over, betray*

11

προφήτης, -ου, ὁ, a prophet (prophet)
σάρξ, σαρκός, ἡ, flesh (sarcophagus, a [stone] coffin which 'eats' [φαγεῖν] the contents)
σύν, with the dat., with (syntax, sentence construction, involving grammatical arrangement [τάσσειν] of words with one another)
σῶμα, -ατος, τό, a body (somatic)
φωνή, -ῆς, a sound, voice (phonetic)

WORDS OCCURRING 101 TO 120 TIMES

ἀγαθός, -ή, -όν, good (Agatha)
ἀγάπη, -ης, ἡ, love
ἀλήθεια, -ας, ἡ, truth
ἀνίστημι, I cause to rise; I arise
ἀπέρχομαι, I depart
ἀποθνῄσκω, I die
βασιλεύς, -έως, ὁ, a king (Basil)
δεῖ, it is necessary
δύναμις, -εως, ἡ, power (dynamite)
ἐκκλησία, -ας, ἡ, assembly, congregation, a church, the Church (ecclesiastic)
ἐξουσία, -ας, ἡ, authority
ζητέω, I seek
θάνατος, -ου, ὁ, death (thanatopsis, a view of, or meditation on, death)
ἴδιος, -α, -ον, one's own (idiosyncrasy)
κρίνω, I judge, decide (critic)
μέλλω, I am about to
μένω, I remain (akin to permanent)
ὁδός, -οῦ, ἡ, a way, road, journey, (anode, cathode, electrical terminals)
οἶκος, -ου, ὁ, a house (economy, household management)
ὅλος, -η, -ον, whole (holocaust)
ὁράω, I see (cf. panorama [πᾶν, all + ὅραμα, a view])
ὅσος, -η, -ον, as great as, as many as
ὅτε, when
παρακαλέω, I beseech, exhort, console (Paraclete, the Comforter, Helper, Advocate, or Counselor)
πῶς, how?
σῴζω, I save (in biochemistry, sozin, any defensive protein in the animal body)
ψυχή, -ῆς, ἡ, soul, life, self (all words beginning with psycho-)

12

ὥρα, -ας, ἡ, an hour (horoscope, prediction based on the observation of the hour of one's birth)

αἷμα, -ατος, τό, blood (anaemia, without blood; haemoglobin)

αἴρω, I take up, take away

ἀλλήλων, of one another (parallel, beside [παρ'] one another)

ἄρτος, -ου, ὁ, bread, a loaf

γεννάω, I beget (cf. hydrogen, so called as being considered the generator of water [ὕδωρ])

διδάσκω, I teach (cf. didactic)

δικαιοσύνη, -ης, ἡ, righteousness

εἰρήνη, -ης, ἡ, peace (Irene)

ἐκεῖ, there

ἐρῶ, I shall say

ἕτερος, -α, -ον, other, another, different (heterodoxy)

θάλασσα, -ης, ἡ, the sea (thalassic)

καλός, -ή, -όν, beautiful, good (kaleidoscope [εἶδος, form + σκοπεῖν, to behold])

οἰκία, -ας, ἡ, a house

οὔτε, neither, nor

ὀφθαλμός, -οῦ, ὁ, an eye (ophthalmology)

περιπατέω, I walk; I live (peripatetics)

πούς, ποδός, ὁ, a foot (podium)

πρῶτος, -η, -ον, first (all words beginning with proto-)

τέκνον, -ου, τό, a child

τίθημι, I place (cf. antithesis)

τόπος, -ου, ὁ, a place (topography, topic)

φοβέομαι, I fear (cf. phobia)

ἀκολουθέω, I follow (cf. acolyte, the assistant who carries the wine and water and the lights at the celebration of the Mass, attending or following the priest)

ἀναβαίνω, I go up (Anabasis)

ἀπόλλυμι, I destroy; middle, I perish (Apollyon, the angel of the bottomless pit, Rev. 9:11)

ἄρχω, I rule; in the New Testament almost always middle, I begin
ἕκαστος, -η, -ον, each
ἐκβάλλω, I cast out
ἐνώπιον, with the gen., before
ἔτι, still, yet, even
κάθημαι, I sit
καιρός, -οῦ, ὁ, time, an appointed time, season
μηδείς, μηδεμία, μηδέν, no one
μήτηρ, μητρός, ἡ, a mother (akin to maternal)
ὅπου, where, whither
πίπτω, I fall
πληρόω, I fill, fulfill
προσέρχομαι, I come to
προσεύχομαι, I pray
ὥστε, so that

WORDS OCCURRING 71 TO 80 TIMES

αἰτέω, I ask
ἀνοίγω, I open
ἀποκτείνω, I kill
ἀπόστολος, -ου, ὁ, an Apostle (Apostle)
βαπτίζω, I baptize (baptize)
δίκαιος, -α, -ον, right, just, righteous
δώδεκα, twelve (dodecagon)
ἐμός, ἐμή, ἐμόν, my, mine
ἑπτά, seven (heptagon)
εὐαγγέλιον, -ου, τό, good news (of the coming of the Messiah), the Gospel (Evangel)
ἱερόν, -οῦ, τό, a temple (cf. hierarchy)
καταβαίνω, I go down
κεφαλή, -ῆς, ἡ, head (cephalic)
μᾶλλον, more, rather
μαρτυρέω, I bear witness, testify (cf. martyr)
πέμπω, I send
πίνω, I drink (cf. potion)
πονηρός, -ά, -όν, evil
πρόσωπον, -ου, τό, face (prosopography, description of the face or personal appearance)

πῦρ, πυρός, τό, fire (pyre)
σημεῖον, -ου, τό, a sign (cf. semaphore, bearing [φέρειν] a sign)
στόμα, -ατος, τό, a mouth (stomach)
τηρέω, I keep
ὕδωρ, ὕδατος, τό, water (hydrophobia; dropsy [formerly hydropsy])
ὑπάγω, I depart
φῶς, φωτός, τό, light (photography, writing [γράφειν] with light)
χαίρω, I rejoice

WORDS OCCURRING 61 TO 70 TIMES

ἀγαπητός, -ή, -όν, beloved
ἄγω, I lead
αἰώνιος, -ον, eternal (aeonian)
ἀπολύω, I release
γραμματεύς, -έως, ὁ, a scribe (cf. grammatical)
δαιμόνιον, -ου, τό, a demon (demon)
δοκέω, I think; seem (Docetism, the early heresy that Christ's body was
    phantasmal or of celestial substance which merely seemed human)
ἐντολή, -ῆς, ἡ, a commandment
ἔξω, without; with the gen., outside
θέλημα, -ατος, τό, will (Monothelite, one who holds that Christ had
    but one will, the divine; condemned by the Sixth General Council,
    A.D. 680)
ἱμάτιον, -ου, τό, a garment
καρπός, -οῦ, ὁ, fruit
κηρύσσω, I proclaim (as a herald, κῆρυξ), preach
νύξ, νυκτός, ἡ, night
ὄρος, ὄρους, τό, a mountain (orology, the scientific study of mountains)
πιστός, -ή, όν, faithful, believing
πλοῖον, -ου, τό, a boat
πρεσβύτερος, -α, -ον, elder (presbyter)
ῥῆμα -ατος, τό, a word (cf. rhetoric)
σάββατον, -ου, τό, the Sabbath (Sabbath)
συνάγω, I gather together (synagogue)
τρεῖς, τρία, three (triad)
φέρω, I carry, bear, lead (Christopher, bearing Christ)
ὧδε, hither, here

ἀρχή, -ῆς, ἡ, a beginning (archaic)
ἀσπάζομαι, I greet, salute
δέχομαι, I receive
διδάσκαλος, -ου, ὁ, a teacher (cf. didactic)
δοξάζω, I glorify (cf. doxology)
ἐπερωτάω, I ask, question, demand of
ἐρωτάω, I ask, request, entreat
ἤδη, now, already
θρόνος, -ου, ὁ, a throne (throne)
κράζω, I cry out
λοιπός, -ή, -όν, remaining; as a noun, the rest; as an adverb, for the rest, henceforth
μέσος, -η, -ον, middle, in the midst (Mesopotamia, in the midst of the rivers [Tigris and Euphrates])
οὐχί (strengthened form of οὐ), not
πλείων, -ονος, larger, more (pleonasm)
προσκυνέω, I worship
συναγωγή, -ῆς, ἡ, a synagogue (synagogue)
τοιοῦτος, -αύτη, -οῦτον and -οῦτο, such
ὑπάρχω, I am, exist; τὰ ὑπάρχοντα, one's belongings
φημί, I say
χαρά, -ᾶς, ἡ, joy, delight

ἄχρι, ἄχρις, with the gen., as far as, up to; as a conjunction, until
γλῶσσα, -ης, ἡ, a tongue, language (glossolalia, the gift of speaking [cf. λαλεῖν] in tongues, 1 Cor. 14)
γραφή, -ῆς, ἡ, a writing, Scripture (Hagiographa, books of the Hebrew Scriptures not included under Law and Prophets)
δεξιός, -ά, -όν, right (opp. left) (akin to dexterous)
διό, wherefore
ἐλπίς, -ίδος, ἡ, hope
ἐπαγγελία, -ας, ἡ, a promise
ἔσχατος, -η, -ον, last (eschatology)
εὐαγγελίζω, I bring good news, preach good tidings (the Gospel) (evangelize)
εὐθύς, straightway, immediately

θεωρέω, I look at, behold (theorem; theory)
λίθος, -ου, ὁ, a stone (monolith; lithograph)
μακάριος, -α, -ον, blessed, happy (macarism, a beatitude)
μηδέ, but not, nor, not even
μόνος, -η, -ον, alone, only (monologue)
ὅπως, in order that, that
παιδίον, -ου, τό, an infant, child
παραβολή, -ῆς, ἡ, a parable (parable)
πείθω, I persuade
σοφία, -ας, ἡ, wisdom (philosophy)
χρόνος, -ου, ὁ, time (chronology)

WORDS OCCURRING 46 TO 49 TIMES

ἁμαρτωλός, -όν, sinful; as a noun, a sinner
ἀπαγγέλλω, I announce, report
ἀποδίδωμι, I give back, pay; middle, I sell
ἄρα, then, therefore
ἔμπροσθεν, with the gen., in front of, before
ἔρημος, -ον, solitary, deserted; as a noun, ἡ ἔρημος, the desert, wilderness
(hermit)
ἔτος, -ους, τό, a year (the Etesian winds in the Mediterranean region
blow annually)
καθίζω, I seat, sit (cf. cathedral, properly, the church which contains
the bishop's chair or seat)
κακός, -ή, -όν, bad, evil (cacophony, discord)
κρατέω, I grasp (cf. plutocratic, grasping wealth [πλοῦτος])
κρίσις, -εως, ἡ, judgment (crisis)
μικρός, -ά, -όν, small, little (microscope; omicron, little 'o')
οὐκέτι, no longer
παραλαμβάνω, I receive
ποῦ, where? whither?
πρό, with the gen., before (prologue)
προσφέρω, I bring to, offer
σπείρω, I sow
σωτηρία, -ας, ἡ, salvation (soteriology)
τρίτος, -η, -ον, third
τυφλός, -ή, -όν, blind (typhlosis, medical term for blindness)
φανερόω, I make manifest

φόβος, -ου, ὁ, fear, terror (phobia)
φυλακή, -ῆς, ἡ, a guard, a prison, a watch
χρεία, -ας, ἡ, a need

<h2 style="text-align:center">WORDS OCCURRING 42 TO 45 TIMES</h2>

ἁμαρτάνω, I sin (cf. hamartiology, the doctrine of sin)
ἀνάστασις, -εως, ἡ, resurrection (Anastasia [girl's name])
ἅπας, -ασα, -αν, all
γενεά, -ᾶς, ἡ, a generation (genealogy)
δεύτερος, -α, -ον, second (Deuteronomy, the second [statement of the] law)
δέω, I bind (diadem, literally, something bound around or across)
διώκω, I pursue, persecute
ἐγγίζω, I come near
ἐπιγινώσκω, I come to know, recognize
εὐλογέω, I bless (eulogize)
θαυμάζω, I marvel, wonder at (cf. thaumaturge, a worker of miracles or wonders)
θεραπεύω, I heal (therapeutic)
θηρίον, -ου, τό, a wild beast (theriomorphic, having animal form; as, theriomorphic gods)
θλῖψις, -εως, ἡ, tribulation
κατοικέω, I inhabit, dwell
λύω, I loose (cf. analysis, a resolving or unloosing into simple elements)
μέρος, -ους, τό, a part (in biology, pentamerous, of five parts)
ναός, -οῦ, ὁ, a temple
ὅμοιος, -α, -ον, like (Homoiousian, one holding that Father and Son in the Godhead are of like [but not the same] substance; a semi-Arian)
σεαυτοῦ, of thyself
σήμερον, today
σπέρμα, -ατος, τό, a seed (sperm)
σταυρόω, I crucify
τιμή, -ῆς, ἡ, honor, price (cf. Timothy, honoring God)
φωνέω, I call (phonetic)

<h2 style="text-align:center">WORDS OCCURRING 38 TO 41 TIMES</h2>

ἄξιος, -α, -ον, worthy (axiom; in philosophy and psychology, axiological, pertaining to the science of values)

ἅπτομαι, I touch
διέρχομαι, I pass through
δικαιόω, I justify, pronounce righteous
ἐπιθυμία, -ας, ἡ, eager desire, passion
ἐπιτίθημι, I lay upon
ἐργάζομαι, I work (cf. energy)
ἑτοιμάζω, I prepare
εὐχαριστέω, I give thanks (Eucharist)
θύρα, -ας, ἡ, a door
ἱκανός, -ή, -όν, sufficient, able, considerable
καινός, -ή, -όν, new
κλαίω, I weep
λογίζομαι, I account, reckon (cf. logic)
μισέω, I hate (misogynist, a woman-hater)
μνημεῖον, -ου, τό, a tomb, monument
οἰκοδομέω, I build, edify
ὀλίγος, -η, -ον, little, few (oligarchy, rule by the few)
οὐαί, woe! alas!
πάντοτε, always
παραγίνομαι, I come, arrive
παρίστημι, I am present, stand by
πάσχω, I suffer
περισσεύω, I abound, am rich
πλανάω, I lead astray (planet, to the ancients, an apparently 'wandering' celestial body)
πράσσω, I do, perform (praxis, practice, as opposed to theory)
πρόβατον, -ου, τό, a sheep
τέλος, -ους, τό, end (teleology, in philosophy, the view that developments are due to the purpose or design [end] that is served by them)
χωρίς, with the gen., without, apart from

WORDS OCCURRING 34 TO 37 TIMES

ἀγρός, -οῦ, ὁ, a field (akin to agrarian)
ἄρτι, now, just now
ἄρχων, -οντος, ὁ, a ruler (monarch, sole [μόνος] ruler)
ἀσθενέω, I am weak
βλασφημέω, I revile, blaspheme (blaspheme)
βούλομαι, I wish, determine (akin to volition)

19

διάβολος, -ον, slanderous, accusing falsely; as a noun, the Accuser, the Devil (diabolical)

διακονέω, I wait upon (especially at table), serve (generally), minister (cf. deacon)

ἐκπορεύομαι, I go out

ἐμαυτοῦ, of myself

ἐπιστρέφω, I turn to, return

εὐθέως, immediately

καλῶς, well

μαρτυρία, -ας, ἡ, a testimony, evidence (cf. martyrdom)

μάρτυς, -υρος, ὁ, a witness (martyr)

μετανοέω, I repent

ὀπίσω, behind, after; with the gen., behind, after (cf. opisthograph, a manuscript written upon both the back and the front, Rev. 5:1)

ὀργή, -ῆς, ἡ, anger

οὖς, ὠτός, τό, an ear (otology)

ὀφείλω, I owe, ought

πειράζω, I test, tempt, attempt

πέντε, five (Pentateuch)

περιτομή, -ῆς, ἡ, circumcision

προσευχή, -ῆς, ἡ, prayer

πτωχός, -ή, -όν, poor; as a noun, a poor man

τέσσαρες, -ων, four (the Diatessaron of Tatian, a harmony of the four Gospels made about A.D. 170; literally, through [the] four)

ὑποστρέφω, I return

ὑποτάσσω, I subject, put in subjection (in grammar, hypotaxis, subordination of clauses)

ὥσπερ, just as, even as

WORDS OCCURRING 32 OR 33 TIMES

ἀναγινώσω, I read

ἀρνέομαι, I deny

βιβλίον, -ου, τό, a book (Bible)

δεικνύω or δείκνυμι, I show (in logic, apodeictic, of clear demonstration)

διαθήκη, -ης, ἡ, a covenant

διακονία, -ας, ἡ, waiting at table, (in a wider sense) service, ministry (diaconate)

δυνατός, -ή, -όν, powerful, possible (cf. dynamite)

ἐγγύς, *near*
ἔξεστι, *it is lawful*
ἐχθρός, -ά, -όν, *hating*; as a noun, *an enemy*
ἥλιος, -ου, ὁ, *the sun* (*helium*)
ἱερεύς, -έως, ὁ, *a priest* (*hier*archy)
καυχάομαι, *I boast*
μέλος, -ους, τό, *a member*
μήτε, *neither, nor*
οἶνος, -ου, ὁ, *wine*
πλῆθος, -ους, τό, *a multitude* (cf. *plethora*)
ποῖος, -α, -ον, *what sort of? what?*
ποτήριον, -ου, τό, *a cup*
συνέρχομαι, *I come together*
ὑπομονή, -ῆς, ἡ, *steadfast endurance*
φυλάσσω, *I guard* (cf. pro*phylactic*)

WORDS OCCURRING 30 OR 31 TIMES

ἀγοράζω, *I buy* (cf. *agora*, the market place)
ἀκάθαρτος, -ον, *unclean*
ἄνεμος, -ου, ὁ, *a wind* (*anemone*; *anemo*meter)
ἀρνίον, -ου, τό, *a lamb*
γε, *indeed, at least, really, even*
διδαχή, -ῆς, ἡ, *teaching* (cf. *didactic*)
ἐλεέω, *I have mercy* (cf. *eleemosynary*; *alms*)
ἐλπίζω, *I hope*
ἐπικαλέω, *I call, name*; middle, *I invoke, appeal to*
ἐπιτιμάω, *I rebuke, warn*
καθαρίζω, *I cleanse* (*catharize*)
ναί, *yea, truly, yes*
ὁμοίως, *likewise*
παραγγέλλω, *I command, charge*
παρέρχομαι, *I pass by, pass away*; *I arrive*
παρρησία, -ας, ἡ, *boldness* (of speech), *confidence*
πλήν, *however, but, only*; with the gen., *except*
σκανδαλίζω, *I cause to stumble* (*scandalize*)
σκότος, -ους, τό, *darkness* (*scoto*scope, a field-glass for seeing by night)
συνείδησις, -εως, ἡ, *conscience*
φαίνω, *I shine, appear* (*phantom*; *phenomenon*)

21

φεύγω, *I flee* (cf. *fugitive*)

φυλή, -ῆς, ἡ, *a tribe* (in zoology, *phylum*, one of the large fundamental divisions of the animal kingdom)

WORDS OCCURRING 28 OR 29 TIMES

ἀληθινός, -ή, -όν, *true*

γαμέω, *I marry* (in biology, *gamete*, a matured germ cell)

γνῶσις, -εως, ἡ, *wisdom* (*gnosis*; *Gnostic*)

διάκονος, -ου, ὁ and ἡ, *a servant, administrator, deacon* (*deacon*)

ἐνδύω, *I put on, clothe*

ἐπεί, *when, since*

ἡγέομαι, *I am chief; I think, regard*

θυσία, -ας, ἡ, *a sacrifice*

ἴδε, *see! behold!*

ἰσχυρός, -ά, -όν, *strong*

ἰσχύω, *I am strong, able*

κρίμα, -ατος, τό, *judgment* (cf. *crisis*)

μάχαιρα, -ης, ἡ, *a sword*

μισθός, -οῦ, ὁ, *wages, reward*

μυστήριον, -ου, τό, *a mystery* (*mystery*)

οὔπω, *not yet*

παράκλησις, -εως, ἡ, *an exhortation, consolation* (cf. *Paraclete*, the Comforter, Helper, Advocate, or Counselor)

πάσχα, indeclinable, τό, *a passover* (*paschal*)

πλούσιος, -α, -ον, *rich* (cf. *pluto*cratic)

πόθεν, *whence?*

ποτέ, *at some time, once, ever*

προσκαλέομαι, *I summon*

προφητεύω, *I prophesy* (cf. *prophet*)

τελέω, *I finish, fulfill* (cf. *tele*ology, in philosophy, the view that developments are due to the purpose or design [τέλος] that is served by them)

φίλος, -η, -ον, *loving*; as a noun, *a friend* (biblio*phile*)

WORDS OCCURRING 26 OR 27 TIMES

ἁγιάζω, *I sanctify* (cf. *hagio*latry, the worship of saints)

ἀδελφή, -ῆς, ἡ, *a sister*

ἀδικία, -ας, ἡ, unrighteousness
ἀληθής, -ές, true
ἀποκαλύπτω, I reveal (apocalypse)
βαστάζω, I bear, carry
ἐκεῖθεν, thence, from that place
ἔλεος, -ους, τό, pity, mercy (cf. eleemosynary; alms)
ἑορτή, -ῆς, ἡ, a feast
ἥκω, I have come
θυγάτηρ, -τρός, ἡ, a daughter
ἰάομαι, I heal (cf. pediatrics, medical care of children [παῖς, παιδός])
καταργέω, I bring to naught, abolish
κελεύω, I order
κώμη, -ης, ἡ, a village
λυπέω, I grieve
νικάω, I conquer (cf. Nicholas, victor over the people [λαός])
ὀμνύω or ὄμνυμι, I swear, take an oath
πόσος, -η, -ον, how great? how much?
σός, σή, σόν, thy, thine
σταυρός, -οῦ, ὁ, a cross
στρατιώτης, -ου, ὁ, a soldier
συνίημι, I understand
φρονέω, I think
χήρα, -ας, ἡ, a widow
χώρα, -ας, ἡ, a country (chorography, describing, or description, of districts)

WORDS OCCURRING 25 TIMES

ἀδικέω, I wrong, do wrong
ἀναβλέπω, I look up, receive sight
γνωρίζω, I make known
δέκα, ten (Decapolis, a league originally consisting of ten Greek cities, mostly SE. of the sea of Galilee)
δένδρον, -ου, τό, a tree (rhododendron, lit. rose-tree)
δουλεύω, I serve
ἕνεκα or ἕνεκεν, with the gen., on account of
καθαρός, -ά, -όν, clean (catharsis)
μανθάνω, I learn (cf. mathematics)
μήποτε, lest perchance

23

νεφέλη, -ης, ἡ, a cloud (nephelometer)
ὁμολογέω, I confess, profess
οὗ, where
πνευματικός, -ή, -όν, spiritual (pneumatic)
πορνεία, -ας, ἡ, fornication (cf. pornography)
προσέχω, I attend to, give heed to
φιλέω, I love (cf. bibliophile)

WORDS OCCURRING 24 TIMES

ἀκοή, -ῆς, ἡ, hearing; a report
ἀναιρέω, I take up; kill
ἀσθένεια, -ας, ἡ, weakness (neurasthenia, nervous prostration)
ἀσθενής, -ές, weak (cf. neurasthenia)
διότι, because
ἐκλεκτός, -ή, -όν, chosen, elect (cf. eclecticism)
ἐπιστολή, -ῆς, ἡ, a letter (epistle)
καταλείπω, I leave
κατηγορέω, I accuse (cf. categorical)
κεῖμαι, I lie, am laid
νοῦς, νοός, ὁ, the mind (noetic)
παῖς, παιδός, ὁ and ἡ, a boy, girl, child, servant (pedagogue, literally,
    child-leader)
πάρειμι, I am present; I have arrived
παρουσία, -ας, ἡ, presence, coming (especially Christ's [second] coming in
    glory) (Parousia)
περιβάλλω, I put around, clothe
πίμπλημι, I fill
σωτήρ, -ῆρος, ὁ, Saviour (cf. soteriology)

WORDS OCCURRING 23 TIMES

ἀμπελών, -ῶνος, ὁ, a vineyard
ἀνάγω, I lead up; middle, I put to sea, set sail
ἄπιστος, -ον, unbelieving, faithless
ἀστήρ, -έρος, ὁ, a star (aster)
αὐξάνω, I cause to grow; increase (cf. auxiliary)
γρηγορέω, I watch (Gregory)
εἰκών, -όνος, ἡ, an image (icon)

24

ἐλεύθερος, -α, -ον, free
ζῷον, -ου, τό, a living creature, an animal (zoology)
θυσιαστήριον, -ου, τό, an altar
κοπιάω, I toil
κωλύω, I forbid, hinder
λευκός, -ή, -όν, white (leukemia, literally, white blood [αἷμα])
μιμνῄσκομαι, I remember (cf. mnemonics)
νέος, -α, -ον, new, young (all words beginning with neo-)
πεινάω, I hunger
πέραν, with the gen., beyond
περισσός, -ή, -όν, excessive, abundant
σκεῦος, -ους, τό, a vessel; plural, goods
τελειόω, I fulfill, make perfect
χαρίζομαι, I give freely, forgive

WORDS OCCURRING 22 TIMES

δέομαι, I beseech
δοκιμάζω, I prove, approve
θεάομαι, I behold (theater)
καθεύδω, I sleep
καθίστημι, I set, constitute
κατεργάζομαι, I work out
κοιλία, -ας, ἡ, the belly (stomach or intestines, or both); womb (coeliac, pertaining to the abdomen)
μετάνοια, -ας, ἡ, repentance
μηκέτι, no longer
νυνί, now
πληγή, -ῆς, ἡ, a blow, wound, plague (plague)
πλοῦτος, -ου, ὁ, wealth (plutocrat)
πωλέω, I sell (cf. monopoly)
στρέφω, I turn (strophe)
συνέδριον, -ου, τό, a council, the Sanhedrin (Sanhedrin)
χιλίαρχος, -ου, ὁ, a military tribune, captain (chiliarch)
ὡσεί, as, like, about

WORDS OCCURRING 21 TIMES

ἀγνοέω, I do not know (agnostic)
ἀντί, with the gen., instead of, for (all words beginning with anti-)

25

ἀργύριον, -ου, τό, silver (in pharmacy, Argyrol, the trade-name of a silver-protein compound)

βασιλεύω, I reign

γένος, -ους, τό, race, kind (akin to genus)

διδασκαλία, -ας, ἡ, teaching

ἑκατοντάρχης (or -αρχος), -ου, ὁ, a centurion

ἐκλέγομαι, I pick out, choose (eclectic)

εὐδοκέω, I think it good, am well pleased with

ἐφίστημι, I stand over, come upon

θερίζω, I reap

λατρεύω, I serve, worship (cf. Mariolatry)

μνημονεύω, I remember (cf. mnemonics)

παράπτωμα, -ατος, τό, a trespass

πειρασμός, -οῦ, ὁ, temptation

τελώνης, -ου, ὁ, a taxgatherer

τεσσαράκοντα, indeclinable, forty

τιμάω, I honor (Timothy, honoring God)

ὑπακούω, I obey

χιλιάς, -άδος, ἡ, a thousand (chiliasm, millenarianism)

WORDS OCCURRING 20 TIMES

αἰτία, -ας, ἡ, a cause, accusation (etiology, the investigation of causes)

ἀκροβυστία, -ας, ἡ, uncircumcision

βάπτισμα, -ατος, τό, baptism (baptism)

γονεύς, -έως, ὁ, a parent (cf. gonad)

ἐνεργέω, I work, effect (cf. energy)

ἐπίγνωσις, -εως, ἡ, knowledge

ἰχθύς, -ύος, ὁ, a fish (ichthyology)

κρύπτω, I conceal (cryptic)

μαρτύριον, -ου, τό, a testimony, witness, proof (cf. martyrdom)

ξύλον, -ου, τό, wood, tree (xylophone)

προάγω, I lead forth, go before

σκηνή, -ῆς, ἡ, a tent, tabernacle (scene)

σοφός, -ή, -όν, wise (cf. sophomore, literally, a wise fool [μωρός])

ὑπηρέτης, -ου, ὁ, a servant, assistant

ὑψόω, I lift up, exalt (cf. hypsophobia, fear of high places)

ἀπέχω, *I have received* (payment); *I am distant*
γεωργός, -οῦ, ὁ, *a farmer* (George)
διακρίνω, *I discriminate, judge*; middle, *I doubt*
δῶρον, -ου, τό, *a gift* (Theodore, Dorothea [or Dorothy], gift of God)
ἐπαίρω, *I lift up*
ἐπάνω, *above*; with the gen., *over*
ἐπιβάλλω, *I lay upon*
ἐπιλαμβάνομαι, *I take hold of*
ἐπουράνιος, -ιον, *heavenly*
ἡγεμών, -όνος, ὁ, *a leader, a* (Roman) *governor* (cf. *hegemony,* leadership, especially of one state of a confederacy)
κοινωνία, -ας, ἡ, *fellowship*; *contribution*
κρείσσων or κρείττων, -ονος, *better*
κριτής, -οῦ, ὁ, *a judge* (*critic*)
κτίσις, -εως, ἡ, *creation, creature*
μεριμνάω, *I am anxious, distracted*
μέχρι or μέχρις, *until*; with the gen., *as far as*
νηστεύω, *I fast*
παλαιός, -ά, -όν, *old* (*palaeography*)
παρατίθημι, *I set before*; middle, *I entrust*
πότε, *when?*
προφητεία, -ας, ἡ, *a prophecy* (*prophecy*)
τέλειος, -α, -ον, *complete, perfect, mature* (cf. *teleology*)
τοσοῦτος, -αύτη, -οῦτον and -οῦτο, *so great, so much*; plural, *so many*
τρέχω, *I run*

ἀληθῶς, *truly*
ἀνάγκη, -ης, ἡ, *necessity*
ἀποκάλυψις, -εως, ἡ, *a revelation* (*apocalypse*)
ἀπώλεια, -ας, ἡ, *destruction* (cf. *Apollyon*)
ἀριθμός, -οῦ, ὁ, *a number* (*arithmetic*)
βλασφημία, -ας, ἡ, *reproach, blasphemy* (*blasphemy*)
δέησις, -εως, ἡ, *an entreaty*
δεσμός, -οῦ, ὁ, *a fetter, bond*
εἰσπορεύομαι, *I enter*

ἐλέγχω, I convict, reprove (elenchus, a logical refutation)
ἐμβαίνω, I embark
ἐπιτρέπω, I permit
θυμός, -οῦ, ὁ, wrath
καταγγέλλω, I proclaim
κατακρίνω, I condemn
κατέχω, I hold back, hold fast
κενός, -ή, -όν, empty, vain (cenotaph, sepulchral monument to a person whose body is not contained in it)
κληρονομέω, I inherit
κοιμάομαι, I sleep, fall asleep (cemetery, literally, a sleeping chamber)
κόπος, -ου, ὁ, labor, trouble
κρυπτός, -ή, -όν, hidden (cryptic)
μήν, μηνός, ὁ, a month (menology, a calendar, especially that of the Greek Church, provided with short biographies of saints)
μήτι, interrogative particle in questions expecting a negative answer
οἰκοδομή, -ῆς, ἡ, a building; edification
παράχρημα, immediately
ποιμήν, -ένος, ὁ, a shepherd (poimenic, pertaining to pastoral theology)
πόλεμος, -ου, ὁ, a war (polemics)
προστίθημι, I add, add to
πυλών, -ῶνος, ὁ, a vestibule, gateway (pylon)
στέφανος, -ου, ὁ, a crown (Stephen)
ταράσσω, I trouble
τίκτω, I give birth to
ὑποκριτής, -οῦ, ὁ, a hypocrite
ὑπομένω, I tarry; I endure
φανερός, -ά, όν, manifest
χρύσεος, -α, -ον, contracted χρυσοῦς, -ῆ, -οῦν, golden (chrysanthemum, literally, golden flower)

WORDS OCCURRING 17 TIMES

ἀρέσκω, I please
αὐτοῦ, of himself
ἄφεσις, -εως, ἡ, a sending away, remission (aphesis, the gradual loss of a short unaccented vowel at the beginning of a word; as 'squire' for 'esquire')
βρῶμα, -ατος, τό, food

28

γάμος, -ov, ό, a marriage, wedding (bigamy, double marriage; digamy, second marriage after the decease of the first spouse, condemned as a sin by certain Church Fathers)

δέσμιος, -ov, ό, a prisoner

ἑκατόν, one hundred (hecatomb, great public sacrifice, properly of 100 oxen [βοῦς])

ἐξίστημι, I amaze, am amazed

ἐπαύριον, on the morrow

ἐπιμένω, I continue

ἕτοιμος, -η, -ov, ready, prepared

θησαυρός, -οῦ, ό, a storehouse, treasure (thesaurus)

ἵππος, -ov, ό, a horse (hippopotamus, literally, a river-horse)

καθάπερ, even as, as

καταλύω, I destroy; I lodge (cf. catalyze)

κερδαίνω, I gain

νίπτω, I wash

νυμφίος, -ov, ό, a bridegroom (akin to nuptial)

περιτέμνω, I circumcize

πλήρωμα, -ατος, τό, fullness (pleroma, in Valentinian Gnosticism, the world of light, including the body of eons)

πλησίον, near; as a noun, a neighbor

πολλάκις, often

ποταμός, -οῦ, ό, a river (hippopotamus, literally, a river-horse)

ῥύομαι, I rescue, deliver

σκοτία, -ας, ή, darkness (scotoscope, a field-glass for seeing by night)

χάρισμα, -ατος, τό, a gift (freely and graciously given) (charism, a special spiritual gift or power divinely conferred; 1 Cor. 12)

ὡσαύτως, likewise

WORDS OCCURRING 16 TIMES

ἀθετέω, I reject (athetize, to reject a text or passage as spurious)

ἀνακρίνω, I examine

ἀπάγω, I lead away

δεῖπνον, -ov, τό, a supper

δηνάριον, -ov, τό, a denarius (denarius)

διαλογίζομαι, I debate

διατάσσω, I command

διψάω, I thirst (cf. dipsomania, a craving for alcohol)

29

ἐκτείνω, I stretch forth (cf. extend)
ἐκχέω, I pour out
ἐντέλλομαι, I command
ἔπειτα, then
ἐπιθυμέω, I desire
ἐργάτης, -ου, ὁ, a workman (cf. energy)
εὐλογία, -ας, ἡ, a blessing (eulogy)
ζῆλος, -ου, ὁ, zeal, jealousy (zeal)
θεμέλιος, -ου, ὁ, a foundation
κακῶς, badly
κατέρχομαι, I come down, go down
κλείω, I shut
κλέπτης, -ου, ὁ, a thief (kleptomaniac)
οὐδέποτε, never
πάθημα, -ατος, τό, suffering (cf. pathological; apathy)
παρέχω, I offer, afford
πέτρα, -ας, ἡ, a rock (petrify)
πλήρης, -ες, full
προσδοκάω, I wait for
ῥαββί, indeclinable, ὁ, (my) master (rabbi)
ῥίζα, -ης, ἡ, a root (cf. rhizome)
συκῆ, -ῆς, ἡ, a fig tree (sycophant, a flatterer, literally, a fig-shower [the
    reason for the name is not definitely known])
συλλαμβάνω, I take, conceive
συνίστημι or συνιστάνω, transitive tenses, I commend; intransitive
    tenses, I stand with, consist
σφραγίς, -ῖδος, ἡ, a seal (sphragistics, the science of seals, their history,
    age, distinctions, etc.)
τέρας, -ατος, τό, a wonder
τολμάω, I dare
τροφή, -ῆς, ἡ, food (cf. atrophy, wasting due to malnutrition)
ὑστερέω, I lack
χορτάζω, I eat to the full, am satisfied, am filled
ὦ, O!

WORDS OCCURRING 15 TIMES

ἀνέχομαι, I endure
γεύομαι, I taste (cf. gusto, disgust)

30

γνωστός, -ή, -όν, known
γυμνός, -ή, -όν, naked (gymnasium)
δέρω, I beat
διαμαρτύρομαι, I testify solemnly
ἐλαία, -ας, ἡ, an olive tree
ἐπαγγέλλομαι, I promise
εὐσέβεια, -ας, ἡ, piety, godliness (Eusebius)
εὐχαριστία, -ας, ἡ, thanksgiving (Eucharist)
θρίξ, τριχός, ἡ, a hair (trichina, a thread-like worm)
καταλαμβάνω, I overtake, apprehend
κατεσθίω, I eat up, devour
κλάω, I break (iconoclast, literally, a breaker of images)
κληρονόμος, -ου, ὁ, an heir
κτίζω, I create
λῃστής, -οῦ, ὁ, a robber
λύπη, -ης, ἡ, pain, grief
μοιχεύω, I commit adultery
νήπιος, -ου, ὁ, an infant, child
νομίζω, I suppose
ξηραίνω, I dry up (cf. xerophagy, among early Christians, the practice of living on a diet of dry food, especially during Lent and other fasts)
ὅθεν, whence, wherefore
οἰκουμένη, -ης, ἡ, the (inhabited) world (cf. ecumenical)
ὁμοιόω, I make like, liken (homoeoteleuton, the occurrence of the same or similar endings of lines, a frequent source of error in copied manuscripts)
παρθένος, -ου, ἡ, a virgin (parthenogenesis)
παύομαι, I cease
ποτίζω, I give drink to (akin to potion)
σαλεύω, I shake
σκάνδαλον, -ου, τό, a cause of stumbling (scandal)
συμφέρω, I bring together; impersonally, it is profitable
σφραγίζω, I seal (cf. sphragistics, the science of seals, their history, age, distinctions, etc.)
τράπεζα, -ης, ἡ, a table (trapeze, so called from the square or rectangle formed by the ropes and crossbar)
τύπος, -ου, ὁ, mark, example (type)
ὑπακοή, -ῆς, ἡ, obedience

31

χόρτος, -ου, ὁ, grass, hay
ὠφελέω, I profit

ἄκανθαι, -ῶν, αἱ, thorns (the acanthus plant)
ἀλλότριος, -α, -ον, another's, strange
ἀμφότεροι, -αι, -α, both
ἀνάκειμαι, I recline (at meals)
ἀναχωρέω, I depart
ἀνθίστημι, I resist
ἀνομία, -ας, ἡ, lawlessness
ἅπαξ, once, once for all
ἀπειθέω, I disbelieve, disobey
ἀτενίζω, I look intently, gaze upon intently
αὔριον, tomorrow
ἀφίστημι, I withdraw, depart
γράμμα, -ατος, τό, a letter (of the alphabet); plural, writings
διαλογισμός, -οῦ, ὁ, a reasoning, questioning (cf. dialogue)
ἕκτος, -η, -ον, sixth
ἐλάχιστος, -η, -ον, least
ἐνιαυτός, -οῦ, ὁ, a year
ἐπίσταμαι, I understand (cf. epistemology, the science of the methods and grounds of knowledge)
εὐφραίνω, I rejoice (cf. Euphrosyne, one of the three Graces in Greek mythology)
κατανοέω, I observe
κληρονομία, -ας, ἡ, an inheritance
κοινός, -ή, -όν, common, unclean (ceremonially)
κοινόω, I make common, I defile (ceremonially) (cf. cenobite, one dwelling in a convent community [where all is held in common])
κωφός, -ή, -όν, deaf, dumb
λύχνος, -ου, ὁ, a lamp
μακρόθεν, from afar, afar
μακροθυμία, -ας, ἡ, long-suffering, patience, forbearance
μερίζω, I divide
μέτρον, -ου, τό, a measure (meter)
μύρον, -ου, τό, ointment
μωρός, -ά, -όν, foolish (moron)

νοέω, I understand (noetic)

ξένος, -η, -ον, strange; as a noun, a stranger, host (the chemical element xenon)

οἷος, -α, -ον, such as

ὄφις, -εως, ὁ, a serpent (Ophites, Gnostics who revered the serpent as the symbol of hidden, divine wisdom)

ὀψία, -ας, ἡ, evening

πετεινά, -ῶν, τά, birds

προσδέχομαι, I receive, wait for

σεισμός, -οῦ, ὁ, an earthquake (seismograph)

σῖτος, -ου, ὁ, wheat (parasite, literally, one who sits by [παρά] another's food and eats at his expense)

στηρίζω, I establish

τάλαντον, -ου, τό, a talent (talent)

ταπεινόω, I humble

φρόνιμος, -η, -ον, prudent

χωλός, -ή, -όν, lame

WORDS OCCURRING 13 TIMES

ἀνά, with the acc., upwards, up; with numerals, each; ἀνὰ μέσον, into the midst, among

ἀναγγέλλω, I announce, report

ἀναλαμβάνω, I take up

ἀναστροφή, -ῆς, ἡ, conduct

ἄνωθεν, from above, again

ἁρπάζω, I seize (cf. harpoon, harpy)

βοάω, I cry aloud

βουλή, -ῆς, ἡ, counsel, purpose

δαιμονίζομαι, I am demon possessed (demonize)

διαλέγομαι, I dispute (dialectics)

διαφέρω, I differ

δράκων, -οντος, ὁ, a dragon (dragon)

εἶτα, then

ἐκπλήσσομαι, I am astonished, amazed

ἐλεημοσύνη, -ης, ἡ, alms (eleemosynary; alms)

ἐμπαίζω, I mock

ἕξ, six (Hexapla, the edition of the Old Testament compiled by Origen, in the third century, comprising six columns)

33

ἐξαποστέλλω, I send forth
ἔξωθεν, with the gen., from without
ἐπιζητέω, I seek for
ἐπιπίπτω, I fall upon
ζύμη, -ης, ἡ, leaven (enzyme)
θερισμός, -οῦ, ὁ, harvest (cf. thermal)
θύω, I sacrifice, kill (thyme)
καπνός, -οῦ, ὁ, smoke
καταισχύνω, I put to shame
κατακαίω, I burn up
καταντάω, I come to
καταρτίζω, I mend, fit, perfect
κλέπτω, I steal (cf. cleptomania)
παιδεύω, I teach, chastise (cf. pedagogue)
παιδίσκη, -ης, ἡ, a maid servant
παράδοσις, -εως, ἡ, a tradition
πρίν, before
πώς, at all, somehow, in any way
συνεργός, -οῦ, ὁ, a fellow worker (cf. synergism, the semi-Pelagian doctrine
    that there are two efficient agents in regeneration, namely the
    human will and the divine Spirit, which, in the strict sense of the
    term, co-operate)
τίμιος, -α, -ον, precious, honorable, (cf. Timothy, honoring God)
τρόπος, -ου, ὁ, manner, way (in rhetoric, trope, a figurative use of a word)
τύπτω, I smite (cf. tympanum, the middle ear)
ὕψιστος, -η, -ον, highest
φύσις, -εως, ἡ, nature (physics)
χρυσίον, -ου, τό, gold (cf. chrysanthemum, literally, golden flower)
χωρίζω, I separate, depart

WORDS OCCURRING 12 TIMES

ἄδικος, -ον, unjust
ἀλέκτωρ, -ορος, ὁ, a cock (cf. alectryomancy, divination by means of a
    cock encircled by grains of corn placed on letters of the alphabet,
    the letters being then put together in the order in which the grains
    were eaten)
ἀναπαύω, I refresh; middle: I take rest
ἀναπίπτω, I recline

34

ἀπαρνέομαι, I deny

ἀσκός, -οῦ, ὁ, a (leather) bottle, wine-skin (in botany, ascidium, the leaf of the pitcher plant)

αὐλή, -ῆς, ἡ, a court (in Austro-German history, the Aulic Council)

βαπτιστής, -οῦ, ὁ, baptist (Baptist)

βασανίζω, I torment

βῆμα, -ατος, τό, judgment seat (in ecclesiastical architecture, bema, the inner part of the chancel, reserved for the clergy)

βροντή, -ῆς, ἡ, thunder (brontosaurus, literally, thunder-lizard)

γέεννα, -ης, ἡ, gehenna (Gehenna)

γόνυ, -ατος, τό, a knee (akin to genuflect)

δεῦτε, come!

διάνοια, -ας, ἡ, the mind, understanding, a thought

δίκτυον, -ου, τό, a net

ἔθος, -ους, τό, a custom (ethics)

ἐξάγω, I lead out

ἐξουθενέω, I despise

ἔσωθεν, from within, within

καίω, I burn (caustic)

κἀκεῖ (= καὶ ἐκεῖ), and there

κάλαμος, -ου, ὁ, a reed (calamus)

κατάκειμαι, I lie down, lie sick, recline (at meals)

κολλάομαι, I join, cleave to (cf. colloid)

κομίζω, I receive

κράτος, -ους, τό, power, dominion (cf. democracy, rule of the people)

λίαν, greatly

λιμός, -οῦ, ὁ, hunger, famine (in medicine, limosis, excessive and morbid hunger)

λυχνία, -ας, ἡ, a lampstand

μάλιστα, especially

ὀδούς, -όντος, ὁ, a tooth (odontology)

οἰκοδεσπότης, -ου, ὁ, a householder

ὅραμα, -ατος, τό, a vision (panorama, a complete [πᾶν] view)

ὅρια, -ων, τά, boundaries (cf. horizon)

παραιτέομαι, I make excuse, refuse

πιάζω, I take

πληθύνω, I multiply

πλουτέω, I am rich (cf. plutocrat)

πόρνη, -ης, ἡ, a prostitute (pornography)

πρόθεσις, -εως, ἡ, a setting forth; a purpose (in the Eastern Church, the prothesis, referring to the placing of the eucharistic elements)
προσλαμβάνω, I receive
πρωΐ, in the morning, early
πῶλος, -ου, ὁ, a colt
ῥάβδος, -ου, ἡ, a staff, rod (rhabdomancy, divination by rods)
σαλπίζω, I sound a trumpet
σπλαγχνίζομαι, I have compassion (splanchnic)
σπουδή, -ῆς, ἡ, haste, diligence
στήκω, I stand, stand fast
συνέχω, I hold fast, oppress
ταχύ, quickly (tachygraphy, stenography, especially that of the ancient Greeks and Romans)
τρίς, thrice (in liturgics, the Trisagion)
τυγχάνω, I obtain, happen
ὑγιαίνω, I am in good health (cf. hygiene)
ὑγιής, -ές, whole, healthy (cf. hygiene)
ὑψηλός, -ή, -όν, high
φιάλη, -ης, ἡ, a cup, bowl (phial, vial)
φονεύω, I kill, murder
χοῖρος, -ου, ὁ, a pig
ψεύδομαι, I lie (pseudo-)

WORDS OCCURRING 11 TIMES

ἀγαλλιάω, I exult
ἀγορά, -ᾶς, ἡ, a market-place (agora)
ἅλυσις, -εως, ἡ, a chain
ἀναστρέφω, I return; I live
ἀπιστία, -ας, ἡ, unbelief
ἀρχαῖος, -α, -ον, old, ancient (archaic)
ἄφρων, -ον, foolish
βρῶσις, -εως, ἡ, eating, food, rust
γέμω, I fill
δάκρυ, -υος, and δάκρυον, -ου, τό, a tear (akin to lachrymal)
διαμερίζω, I divide, distribute
δόλος, -ου, ὁ, guile
δωρεά, -ᾶς, ἡ, a gift
ἐάω, I permit

εἴδωλον, -ου, τό, an image, idol (idol)
εἴκοσι, twenty (icosahedron, a geometric figure with twenty faces)
εἰσάγω, I lead in
ἐκχύννομαι, I pour out
ἔλαιον, -ου, τό, olive-oil (akin to oil, oleo-)
ἐλευθερία, -ας, ἡ, liberty
ἐμβλέπω, I look at
ἐνδείκνυμαι, I show forth
ἔπαινος, -ου, ὁ, praise
ἐπαισχύνομαι, I am ashamed
ἐπισκέπτομαι, I visit, have a care for (cf. episcopal)
ζηλόω, I am zealous (cf. zeal)
ζῳοποιέω, I make alive
θανατόω, I put to death (cf. thanatopsis)
θάπτω, I bury (cf. cenotaph; epitaph)
κακία, -ας, ἡ, malice, evil
καταβολή, -ῆς, ἡ, a foundation (cf. katabolism)
κατασκευάζω, I prepare
κάτω, down, below
καύχημα, -ατος, τό, a boasting, ground of boasting
καύχησις, -εως, ἡ, boasting
κέρας, -ατος, τό, horn (rhinoceros, literally, nose-horn)
κλάδος, -ου, ὁ, a branch (of a tree) (in botany, cladophyll)
κλῆρος, -ου, ὁ, a lot (that which is cast or drawn); a portion (clergy; cleric, clerk)
κλῆσις, -εως, ἡ, a (divine) call, invitation, summons
κλητός, -ή, -όν, called
κράβαττος, -ου, ὁ, a mattress, pallet, bed (of a poor man)
λίμνη, -ης, ἡ, a lake (limnology, the scientific study of ponds and lakes)
μεταβαίνω, I depart
νεανίσκος, -ου, ὁ, a youth
νόσος, -ου, ἡ, a disease (nosophobia, a morbid fear of disease)
ὁμοθυμαδόν, with one accord
ὀνειδίζω, I reproach
παράγω, I pass by
παραλυτικός, -οῦ, ὁ, a paralytic (paralytic)
παρεμβολή, -ῆς, ἡ, a camp, army, fortress
περισσοτέρως, more abundantly
πηγή, -ῆς, ἡ, a spring, fountain

37

ποιμαίνω, I shepherd, rule (poimenic, pertaining to pastoral theology)
πρᾶγμα, -ατος, τό, a deed, matter, thing (pragmatic)
πραΰτης, -ῆτος, ἡ, gentleness, humility, courtesy
πρότερος, -α, -ον, former; as an adverb, before (cf. proto-)
πυνθάνομαι, I inquire
σάλπιγξ, -ιγγος, ἡ, a trumpet
σπλάγχνα, -ων, τά, bowels; heart, tender mercies, compassion (splanchnic)
σπουδάζω, I hasten, am eager
σφόδρα, exceedingly
σχίζω, I split (schism; schizophrenia)
τελευτάω, I die
τριάκοντα, indeclinable, thirty
ὑμέτερος, -α, -ον, your
ὑπαντάω, I meet, go to meet
ὑποκάτω, under, below, down at
ὕστερον, later, afterwards (in rhetoric, hysteron-proteron, a reversing of
   the natural order of the sense, as 'he is well and lives')
φυτεύω, I plant
φωτίζω, I give light, enlighten (cf. photo-)
χείρων, -ον, worse, more severe
χίλιοι, -αι, -α, a thousand (chiliasm, millenarianism)
χιτών, -ῶνος, ὁ, a tunic (chiton)
χράομαι, I use (catachresis, misuse of a word; in rhetoric, a mixed
   metaphor)
χρυσός, -οῦ, ὁ, gold (chrysanthemum)
ψευδοπροφήτης, -ου, ὁ, a false prophet

WORDS OCCURRING 10 TIMES

ἁγιασμός, -οῦ, ὁ, sanctification
ᾅδης, -ου, ὁ, Hades (Hades)
ἀδύνατος, -ον, incapable, impossible
ἀκαθαρσία, -ας, ἡ, uncleanness
ἅμα, at the same time; with the dat., together with
ἀνατολή, -ῆς, ἡ, east, dawn (Anatolia)
ἀναφέρω, I bring up, offer
ἄνομος, -ον, lawless, without law
ἀπολογέομαι, I defend myself (cf. apology)
ἀπολύτρωσις, -εως, ἡ, redemption

ἀσέλγεια, -ας, ἡ, licentiousness, debauchery, sensuality

ἀσπασμός, -οῦ, ὁ, a greeting

ἀφαιρέω, I take away (aphaeresis, dropping of a letter or syllable from the beginning of a word, as 'lone' from 'alone')

ἀφορίζω, I separate (aphorism)

βίβλος, -ου, ἡ, a book (Bible)

βίος, -ου, ὁ, life (biology)

δεσπότης, -ου, ὁ, a master, lord (despot)

διατρίβω, I continue (diatribe, a prolonged and acrimonious harangue)

δικαίωμα, -ατος, τό, regulation, righteous deed

διωγμός, -οῦ, ὁ, persecution

ἐγκαταλείπω, I leave behind, forsake, abandon

ἐκκόπτω, I cut out, cut off

ἐκπίπτω, I fall away

ἐμφανίζω, I manifest

ἔνατος, -η, -ον, ninth (Ennead, one division of the collection made by Porphyry of the teachings of Plotinus, arranged in six divisions of nine books each)

ἔνοχος, -ον, involved in, liable, guilty

ἐξομολογέομαι, I confess, profess (in the ancient Church, exomologesis, the public confession of sin, usually accompanied by fasting, weeping, and mourning)

ἐπειδή, since, because

ἐπιδίδωμι, I give to

ἐπιτάσσω, I command

ἐπιτελέω, I complete, perform

θλίβω, I press, oppress

ἰσχύς, -ύος, ἡ, strength

κἀκεῖθεν (= καὶ ἐκεῖθεν), and from there; and then

κοινωνός, -οῦ, ὁ, a partner, sharer (cf. cenobite, one dwelling in a convent community)

κοσμέω, I adorn (cosmetics)

μακράν, far away

μακροθυμέω, I am patient

μέλει, it is a care

μνῆμα, -ατος, τό, grave, tomb

νομικός, -ή, -όν, pertaining to the law; as a noun, one skilled in the Mosaic law, a lawyer

ξενίζω, I entertain (a stranger); I startle, bewilder

ὅδε, ἥδε, τόδε, this (here)
οἰκονόμος, -ου, ὁ, a steward (economy)
ὀνομάζω, I name (cf. onomasticon, a collection of proper names)
ὄντως, really (cf. ontology)
ὅρκος, -ου, ὁ, an oath
παντοκράτωρ, -ορος, ὁ, ruler of all, the Almighty
πατάσσω, I smite
πενθέω, I mourn
περιστερά, -ᾶς, ἡ, a dove
πλάνη, -ης, ἡ, a wandering, error (cf. planet, which to the ancients was
    apparently a wandering celestial body)
πλατεῖα, -ας, ἡ, a street (place)
πλεονεξία, -ας, ἡ, covetousness
ποικίλος, -η, -ον, varied, manifold
πόρνος, -ου, ὁ, a fornicator (pornography)
προέρχομαι, I go in front, precede
προσκαρτερέω, I continue in or with
πύλη, -ης, ἡ, a gate, porch (pylon)
σέβομαι, I reverence, worship
σιγάω, I am silent, become silent
σιωπάω, I am silent (aposiopesis, in rhetoric, a figure of speech in which
    the speaker breaks off suddenly)
στρατηγός, -οῦ, ὁ, a commander
συγγενής, -ές, kindred; as a noun, a relative, kinsman
συζητέω, I discuss, dispute
σύνδουλος, -ου, ὁ, a fellow slave
σφάζω, I slay
τάσσω, I arrange, appoint, order (cf. tactics)
ταχέως, quickly (cf. tachygraphy)
τέταρτος, -η, -ον, fourth (cf. tetrarch, a ruler over a fourth part)
ὑπόδημα, -ατος, τό, a sandal, shoe
φείδομαι, I spare
χρηστότης, -ητος, ἡ, goodness, kindness
χωρίον, -ου, τό, a place, field (cf. chorography, describing, or description,
    of districts)
ψεῦδος, -ους, τό, a lie (cf. pseudo-)
ψεύστης, -ου, ὁ, a liar (cf. pseudo-)

PART II

WORDS CLASSIFIED ACCORDING TO THEIR ROOT

AFTER the student has mastered about four or five hundred words of frequent occurrence in the Greek Testament, he can begin to use with profit the following groups of words arranged according to their root. Here are collected those words, scattered throughout Part I, which are related to each other by reason of a common etymology. Each group was formed in accord with the requirement that it must contain at least three words each of which occurs ten or more times in the New Testament. In addition to the words from Part I that satisfy this arbitrary requirement, there have been added about 250 other words, each of which occurs from five to nine times in the New Testament. It will be discovered that these words of comparatively infrequent occurrence can be learned with very little additional effort when they are thus grouped with others derived from the same root.

THE FORMATION OF WORDS

Words do not grow haphazardly or in isolation from the rest of the vocabulary. To see how verbs, nouns, adjectives, adverbs, and particles can be traced to a relatively few basic roots is not only a fascinating study in itself, but it also lessens the drudgery of piecemeal memorization of individual words. Thus, for example, from the root *TEΛ*, meaning *end*, is formed the noun τέλος with the same meaning. From the noun a verb is produced, τελέω, meaning *I finish* or *fulfill* (that is, *I make an appropriate end*). From the noun comes also the adjective τέλειος, meaning *complete, perfect, mature* (that is, *brought to its appropriate end*). The adjective, again, is made into the verb τελειόω, which means *I complete, make perfect*—being equivalent to τέλειον ποιέω. Moreover, the same root *TEΛ* appears in τελευτάω, a verb formed ultimately from τέλος and which means *I die* (that is, *I come to the end [of my life]*). Finally, to complete the list of all the words from this root which appear in the New Testament five times or more, by composition with prepositions the compound words ἐπιτελέω, συντέλεια, and συντελέω are formed, each of which involves some aspect of the root idea of *end*.

This example illustrates the principle of the building of Greek words. The root is the primitive part of the word; it conveys the basic meaning or idea. From the root are produced various verb-stems and noun-stems (the latter of which produce both nouns and adjectives). These stems are built (1) by the addition of various suffixes and/or (2) by the internal modification of the stem. The following is a simplified classification of some of the more important ways in which the words of the Greek Testament are formed. For a more complete technical description, any large reference grammar of New Testament Greek should be consulted.[1]

The suffix is a formative element standing between the root and the declensional or conjugational ending. Suffixes limit or particularize the basic meaning of the root. Some suffixes[2] have special meanings, and when these are known it is often possible to deduce the general significance of an unfamiliar Greek word by analyzing the root idea in the stem as qualified by the suffix.

A. *Suffixes forming nouns*

The following suffixes are listed with the ending of the nominative case, singular number, attached. The numeral within the parentheses following the suffix indicates the declension of the nouns formed with that suffix.

    1. The *agent* is indicated by -της (1).

Examples: βαπτισ-τής (from βαπτίζω), *one who baptizes, a baptizer, baptist*

           μαθη-τής (from μανθάνω), *one who learns, a learner, disciple*

    2. An *action* is indicated by -μος (2) and -σις (3). The latter suffix often produces the abstract name of an action.

---

[1] The best treatment is that by J. H. Moulton and W. F. Howard, *A Grammar of New Testament Greek*, vol. ii, *Accidence and Word-Formation* (Edinburgh, 1929), pp. 268–410.

[2] It should be noted that roots, stems, and suffixes never existed as independent words in Greek, or indeed in any known period of the parent language from which Greek and the other Indo-European tongues were derived. The analysis of words into their component morphological elements is merely a scientific device useful for purposes of arrangement and classification.

Examples: βαπτισ-μός (from βαπτίζω), *a washing, purification* (the act of which βάπτισμα is the result; see below)

καθαρισ-μός (from καθαρίζω), *a cleansing, purification*

ἀπολύτρω-σις (from ἀπολυτρόω, *I release on payment of a ransom*), *a releasing effected by payment of a ransom* (λύτρον), *redemption*

δικαίω-σις (from δικαιόω), *an act of adjudging one to be righteous, justification*

3. The *result* of an action is indicated by -μα (3).

Examples: βάπτισ-μα (from βαπτίζω), *baptism* (the abiding fact resulting from the act of baptism; see above, βαπτισμός)

γράμ-μα (from γράφω), *thing written, a letter* (of the alphabet)

κήρυγ-μα (from κηρύσσω), *thing proclaimed by a herald, preaching*

4. The abstract idea of *quality* is indicated by -ια (1), -οτης (3), and -συνη (1).

Examples: σοφ-ία, *wisdom*

σωτηρ-ία, *salvation*

κυρι-ότης, *lordship, dominion*

νε-ότης, *youth*

ἀγαθω-σύνη, *goodness*

δικαιο-σύνη, *righteousness*

B. Suffixes forming adjectives

1. Adjectives expressing the meaning *of* or *belonging to* a person or thing are formed by adding the suffix -ιος to a noun-stem.

Examples: οὐράν-ιος, *heavenly* (from οὐρανός, *heaven*)

πλούσ-ιος, *wealthy* (from πλοῦτος, *wealth*)

τίμ-ιος, *precious, honorable* (from τιμή, *honor, price*)

2. Adjectives expressing the idea *belonging to, pertaining to, with the characteristics of*, are formed by adding the suffix -ικος to a noun-stem.

Examples: βασιλ-ικός, *belonging to a king, kingly, royal* (from βασιλεύς, *a king*)

πνευματ-ικός, *pertaining to the spirit, with the characteristics of the spirit, spiritual* (from πνεῦμα, *spirit*)

σαρκ-ικός, *fleshly, carnal* (from σάρξ, *flesh*)

σωματ-ικός, *pertaining to the body, bodily* (from σῶμα, *body*)

43

3. Adjectives which express the *material* from which anything is made are formed with the suffix -ινος.

Examples: δερμάτ-ινος, *of skin, leathern*
δλίθ-ινος, *of stone*
σάρκ-ινος, *of the flesh*

4. Many other adjectival suffixes have no characteristic signification. Some of these are -ος, -λος, -νος, -ανος, -μος, and -ρος.

5. A special class of adjectives, called verbal adjectives, is formed by the suffix -τος. These either (*a*) have the meaning of a perfect passive participle or (*b*) express *possibility*.

Examples: (*a*) ἀγαπη-τός, *beloved*
εὐλογη-τός, *blessed*
κρυπ-τός, *hidden*
(*b*) ἀνεκ-τός, *bearable, tolerable*

In general the passive sense is more common. Some have either signification, as ἀδύνα-τος, *incapable* or *impossible*.

C. *Suffixes forming verbs*

From the original verb-stem, which is ordinarily preserved unchanged in the second aorist stem, the present stem is formed in various ways, some of which are the following. It will be observed that not only are suffixes employed but also an internal modification of the stem may take place (called *Ablaut*).

1. The verb-stem may remain unchanged.

Examples: ἄγ-ω, *I lead*
δέ-ω, *I bind*
λύ-ω, *I loose*

2. The initial consonant of the verb-stem may undergo reduplication.

Examples: γίνομαι, *I become*, from the stem γεν- (classical γίγνομαι, from *γι-γέν-ομαι)[1]
δί-δω-μι, *I give*, from the stem δο-
ἵ-στη-μι *I cause to stand*, from the stem στα- (for *σί-στη-μι)
πίπτω, *I fall*, from the stem πετ- (for *πι-πέτ-ω)

[1] An asterisk preceding a Greek word here and in the list below signifies that the word, though preserved in no extant source, must be postulated as the parent of existing forms.

44

3. The vowel in the verb-stem may be lengthened.

Examples: λείπ-ω, *I leave*, from λιπ- (cf. 2nd aor. ἔ-λιπ-ον)
πείθ-ω, *I persuade*, from πιθ- (cf. 2nd aor. ἔ-πιθ-ον)
φεύγ-ω, *I flee*, from φυγ- (cf. 2nd aor. ἔ-φυγ-ον)

4. The final consonant of the verb-stem may be doubled.

Examples: ἀπο-στέλλ-ω, *I send away*, from στελ-
βάλλ-ω, *I throw*, from βαλ- (cf. 2nd aor. ἔ-βαλ-ον)

5. Another consonant may be added to the verb-stem, as -ν-, -σκ-, or -τ-.

Examples: θνή-σκω, *I die*, from θαν- (cf. 2nd aor. ἔ-θαν-ον)
πί-νω, *I drink*, from πι- (cf. 2nd aor. ἔ-πι-ον)
τύπ-τω, *I strike*, from τυπ- (cf. 2nd aor. ἔ-τυπ-ον)

6. An additional syllable may be added to the verb-stem.

(*a*) The ending -άνω, sometimes with ν (μ before a labial) inserted in the verb-stem, may be added.

Examples: ἁμαρτ-άνω, *I sin*, from ἁμαρτ- (cf. 2nd aor. ἥμαρτ-ον)
μανθ-άνω, *I learn*, from μαθ- (cf. 2nd aor. ἔ-μαθ-ον)

(*b*) The endings -άζω, -ίζω, or -ύζω may be added.

Examples: λιθ-άζω, *I stone*
ἐλπ-ίζω, *I hope*
γογγ-ύζω, *I grumble, murmur*

(*c*) The endings -άω, -έω, or -εύω may be added. These usually denote an action or state similar to that expressed by the noun-stem.

Examples: ἀγαπ-άω, *I love*, from ἀγάπη, *love*
δουλ-εύω, *I serve (as a slave)*, from δοῦλος, *a slave*
φιλ-έω, *I love, am friendly towards*, from φίλος, *a friend*

(*d*) The endings -αίνω, -όω, or -ύνω may be added. These usually express causation, except in verbs of mental action such as ἀξι-όω, *I deem worthy*, δικαι-όω, *I deem or judge or pronounce righteous*.

Examples: δουλ-όω, *I enslave*, from δοῦλος, *a slave*
πικρ-αίνω, *I make bitter, embitter*, from πικρός, *sharp, bitter*
πληθ-ύνω, (transitive) *I multiply*, (intransitive) *I abound*,
from πλῆθος, *a multitude*

45

(e) Some Greek verbs are 'irregular,' that is, their present stem is entirely different from their aorist stem (and frequently other stems likewise). Thus, φέρω means *I carry*, but ἤνεγκα means *I carried*; ἐσθίω means *I eat*, ἔφαγον means *I ate*. The reason for the existence of these irregular verbs is simply that the aorist tense of one verb and the present tense of another verb of quite similar meaning both fell into disuse. The remaining present and aorist tenses of these two verbs then came to be associated together as though they were related etymologically. The same thing has happened in languages other than Greek. In English the verb *went* is not the etymological preterit of *go*; it is the past tense of the little-used verb *wend*. Further, modern English rejects the earlier preterit of *go* (the Anglo-Saxon *eode* and Middle English *yode*). The tenses that remain of each verb now function as the principal parts of one verb. In French, to take an example of irregularity within the same tense, the first and second persons plural of the present tense of the verb *aller*, 'to go,' are *nous allons, vous allez*, but the other forms of the present tense are *je vais, tu vas*, etc. The conjugation of the verb is irregular because behind the different forms lie two different Latin words which, for some reason, came to be preferred in those persons (they are *ambulare* and *vadare*, both meaning 'to walk, go').[1]

The irregular verbs which (with their compounds) occur most frequently in the Greek New Testament are the following. A hyphen before a principal part means that this form appears only in compound verbs.

αἱρέω, *I take*, middle, *I choose*, fut. αἱρήσομαι and -ελῶ, 2nd aor. -εῖλον, middle εἱλάμην, perf. -ῄρημαι, aor. passive -ῃρέθην.

εἶπον and εἶπα, *I said*, fut. ἐρῶ, perf. εἴρηκα, perf. passive εἴρημαι, aor. passive ἐρρέθην and ἐρρήθην.

ἔρχομαι, *I come, go*, fut. ἐλεύσομαι, 2nd aor. ἦλθον, perf. ἐλήλυθα.

ἐσθίω and ἔσθω, *I eat*, fut. φάγομαι, 2nd aor. ἔφαγον.

ὁράω, *I see*, fut. ὄψομαι, 2nd aor. εἶδον, perf. ἑώρακα and ἑόρακα, aor. passive ὤφθην.

τρέχω, *I run*, 2nd aor. ἔδραμον.

φέρω, *I carry*, fut. οἴσω, aor. ἤνεγκα and -ήνεγκον, perf. -ενήνοχα, aor. passive ἠνέχθην.

---

[1] The Italian verb *andare* exhibits the same irregularity: *noi andiamo, voi andate*, but *io vado, tu vai*, etc.

Everything set forth above refers to the building of simple words from one stem. Compound words, on the other hand, are formed from a union of two or more stems or parts, as ψευδο-προφήτης, *a false prophet*, and ἀντι-παρ-ῆλθεν, *he passed by* [παρά] *on the other side* [ἀντί], used of the priest and the Levite in the parable of the Good Samaritan (Luke 10: 31 f.). As can be observed from these two examples, a compound word contains a defining part and a defined part, usually in this order. The parts of a compound word stand in various syntactical relations to each other, as that of adjective or attributive genitive to a noun, or that of adverb or object to a verb, etc. Compounds may thus be regarded as abbreviated forms of syntax. In analyzing the meaning of a compound, it must be kept in mind that no part of the word is without significance.

Compound words are formed chiefly in the following three ways.

1. Various particles and adverbs may be prefixed. The two of most frequent occurrence are:

(*a*) The alpha privative, ἀ- (before vowels generally ἀν-), which gives a negative sense to the word to which it is affixed (cf. the English prefix 'un-').

Examples: ἄ-δικος, *unjust*
ἀ-τιμάζω, *I dishonor*
ἀν-έγκλητος, *unreprovable, blameless*

(*b*) The adverbial prefix εὐ-, which supplies the general idea of 'prosperously,' 'being well disposed.'

Examples: εὐ-δοκέω, *I am well pleased, think it good*
εὐ-λογέω, *I speak well of, praise, bless*

2. One or more prepositions may be prefixed. For detailed information concerning this very large class of compound verbs, see Appendix II.

3. Two or more noun-stems or verb-stems may be compounded. As regards their meaning, compound nouns (substantives and adjectives) may be divided into two principal classes.

(*a*) Objective compounds. In these the first part is related to the other as a kind of grammatical object. When the two are expressed

47

in English as separate words, the first is put in an oblique case depending, either immediately or by means of a preposition, on the other.

Examples: θεό-πνευστος, *inspired by God*
νομο-διδάσκαλος, *a teacher of* [*the*] *Law*
οἰκο-δεσπότης, *a master of a house, a householder*

(*b*) Possessive and descriptive compounds. In these the first part qualifies the second as an adjective or adverb.

Examples: μακρο-θυμία, *long-suffering*
μον-όφθαλμος, *one-eyed, having one eye*
ὀλιγό-πιστος, *having little faith*
ταπεινο-φροσύνη, *lowliness of mind, humility*

In drawing up the following ninety-six groups of words the author has tried to avoid two extremes. He has tried to refrain from spinning out fanciful derivations for the sake of establishing connections between words which, according to scientific linguistics, are entirely unrelated. No statement about root or derivation is made which involves a descent to the level of popular or folk-etymology. If a root is obscure or uncertain—or even merely probable—it has not been given.[1] The other extreme which he has tried to avoid is the cumbering of the lists with technical details of advanced linguistics. It may very well be, for example, that originally there was but one root ΛΕΓ which meant 'gather, pick' as well as 'say,' but it is not inaccurate to differentiate between the two by forming two separate lists of words involving each of these meanings; and certainly such an arrangement is less liable to engender confusion than the other.

Finally, it ought to be mentioned that several of the roots contain the obsolete Greek letter *vau*, ϝ, called 'digamma' (i.e. *double-gamma*) from its shape.[2] The sound of this letter was like that of English *w*. Thus, the root ϜΙΔ, 'see,' lies behind εἶδον (for ἐ-ϝιδ-ον) and the second perfect tense οἶδα, *I know* (literally, *I have seen*); compare other Indo-

[1] The chief authorities upon which the etymologies are based are Walther Prellwitz, *Etymologisches Wörterbuch der griechischen Sprache*, 2nd edn. (Göttingen, 1905), and Émile Boisacq, *Dictionnaire étymologique de la langue grecque*, 3rd edn. (Heidelberg and Paris, 1938).

[2] *Vau* had not entirely disappeared in pronunciation when the Homeric epics were composed, and not a few apparent irregularities of meter in these poems can be explained by postulating its influence. For a discussion of the letter, see Edgar H. Sturtevant, *The Pronunciation of Greek and Latin*, 2nd edn. (Philadelphia, 1940), pp. 65–8, and W. Sidney Allen, *Vox Graeca* (Cambridge, 1968), pp. 45–50.

European words, such as Sanskrit *ved-a*, 'knowledge'; Latin *vid-eo*, 'I see'; German *wis-sen*, 'know'; Anglo-Saxon *wit-an* (English *to wit* and the archaic *wot* [means 'know'; see Acts 3 : 17, Rom. 11 : 2, etc., in the King James Version]).

root ΆΓ, 'drive, lead, weigh'

ἄγω, *I lead*

ἀνάγω, *I lead up*; middle, *I put to sea, set sail*

ἀπάγω, *I lead away*

εἰσάγω, *I lead in, bring in*

ἐξάγω, *I lead out*

παράγω, *I pass by*

περιάγω, *I lead about, go about*

προάγω, *I lead forth, go before*

συνάγω, *I gather together*

συναγωγή, -ῆς, *a synagogue*

ἀρχισυνάγωγος, -ου, ὁ, *a ruler of a synagogue*

ἐπισυνάγω, *I collect, gather together at one place*

ὑπάγω, *I depart*

ἀγρός, -οῦ, ὁ, (place where cattle are *led* or *driven*), *a field*

ἡγέομαι, *I am chief*; (*I lead through the mind*), *I think, regard*

ἡγεμών, -όνος, ὁ, *a leader, governor*

ἄξιος, -α, -ον, (*of equal weight*), *worthy*

ἀξιόω, *I deem worthy, think fit*

ἀξίως, *worthily*

ἀγών, -ῶνος, ὁ, *an athletic contest, a contest*

root ΆΓ, 'religious awe, reverence'

ἅγιος, -α, -ον, *holy*

ἁγιάζω, *I make holy, sanctify*

ἁγιασμός, -οῦ, ὁ, *sanctification*

ἁγνός, -ή, -όν, (in a condition prepared for worship), *pure* (ethically, ritually, or ceremonially), *chaste*

ἁγνίζω, *I make pure*

ἀγαπάω, I love
ἀγάπη, -ης, ἡ, love
ἀγαπητός, -ή, -όν, beloved

_____

ἄγγελος, -ου, ὁ, a messenger, an angel
ἀναγγέλλω, I announce, report
ἀπαγγέλλω, I announce, report
ἐπαγγελία, -ας, ἡ, a promise
ἐπαγγέλλομαι, I promise
εὐαγγελίζω, I bring good news, preach good tidings (the Gospel)
εὐαγγέλιον, -ου, τό, good news, the Gospel
καταγγέλλω, I proclaim
παραγγέλλω, I command, charge
παραγγελία, -ας, ἡ, a command

_____

αἰτέω, I ask
αἰτία, -ας, ἡ, a cause, accusation
παραιτέομαι, I make excuse, refuse

_____

ἀκούω, I hear
εἰσακούω, I hearken to, assent to
ὑπακούω, I obey
ἀκοή, -ῆς, ἡ, hearing, a report
ὑπακοή, -ῆς, ἡ, obedience

root ΑΛΛ, 'other'

ἄλλος, -η, -ο, other, another
ἀλλήλων, (reduplicated stem, αλλ-ηλο), of one another
ἀλλά, (neuter plural with changed accent: 'in another way'), but
ἀλλάσσω, (I make other than it is), I change, alter
καταλλάσσω, I change (from enmity to friendship), reconcile

root ΑΡ, 'join, fit'

ἀρέσκω, (I fit or join together; suit), I please
ἀριθμός, -οῦ, ὁ, a number
ἄρτι, (fitting exactly), now, just now
ἀρετή, -ῆς, ἡ, (moral fitness), virtue, excellence

root ΑΡΧ, 'be first'

ἄρχω, (*first* in point of station), *I rule*; middle, (*first* in point of time),
   I begin
ἄρχων, -οντος, ὁ, *a ruler*
ἀρχή, -ῆς, ἡ, *a beginning*
ἀρχαῖος, -α, -ον, *old, ancient*
ἀρχιερεύς, -έως, ὁ, *a chief priest, high priest*
ὑπάρχω, (*I am under* as a foundation, support), *I am, I exist, I belong to*
   (τὰ ὑπάρχοντα, one's *belongings, possessions*)
ἀπαρχή, -ῆς, ἡ, *first fruits*

root ΒΑ, 'go'

ἀναβαίνω, *I go up*
ἐμβαίνω, (*I step into* [a boat]), *I embark*
ἐπιβαίνω, *I go up to, mount, board* (a boat)
καταβαίνω, *I go down*
μεταβαίνω, *I depart*
παράβασις, -εως, ἡ, (*a going over* [the line]), *transgression, a transgression*
παραβάτης, -ου, ὁ, *a transgressor*
προβαίνω, *I go forward, go on*
πρόβατον, -ου, τό, *a sheep* (that which *goes forward*)
συμβαίνω, (of events) *happen, occur*
βῆμα, -ατος, τό, *judgment seat* (that which the judge *mounts*)
βέβαιος, -α, -ον, (reduplicated stem, βε-βα-, *standing fast*), *solid, sure,*
   firm
βεβαιόω, *I confirm, ratify*
βέβηλος, -η, -ον, (lawful to be *trodden*), *profane, secular*

root ΒΑΛ, 'throw'

βάλλω, *I throw, put*
ἐκβάλλω, *I cast out*
ἐπιβάλλω, *I lay upon*
λιθοβολέω, *I pet with stones, kill by stoning*
περιβάλλω, *I put around, clothe*
συμβάλλω, (*I throw together*), *I encounter, meet, consider*; middle, *contribute to*
ὑπερβάλλω, (*I surpass in throwing*), *I surpass, exceed*
διάβολος, -ου, ὁ, (*one who throws across* or *at*, with words, *a slanderer*), *the*
   accuser, the Devil
καταβολή, -ῆς, -ή, (*that which is put down*), *a foundation*

παραβολή, -ῆς, ἡ (*a placing of one thing by the side of another, by way of comparison*), *a parable*
παρεμβολή, -ῆς, ἡ, *a camp, army, fortress*
ὑπερβολή, -ῆς, ἡ, (*a throwing beyond*), *excess, abundance*

βασιλεύς, -έως, ὁ, *a king*
βασιλεύω, *I reign*
βασιλεία, -ας, ἡ, *a kingdom*
βασιλικός, -ή, -όν, *kingly, royal*

root ΒΑΦ, 'dip'

βαπτίζω, *I baptize*
βάπτισμα, -ατος, τό, *baptism*
βαπτιστής, -οῦ, ὁ, *baptizer, Baptist* (used only of John)

βλέπω, *I see*
ἀναβλέπω, *I look up, receive sight*
ἐμβλέπω, *I look at*
περιβλέπομαι, *I look around, survey*

root ΓΕΝ, 'beget, become'

γίνομαι, (Attic, γίγνομαι, a reduplicated form, = *γι-γέν-ομαι), *I become, come into being, happen, am made, am*
παραγίνομαι, *I come, arrive*
γονεύς, -έως, ὁ, *a parent*
γένος, -ους, τό, *race, kind*
μονογενής, -ές, *only, unique, only-begotten*
συγγενής, -ές, *related; a relative, kinsman*
γενεά, -ᾶς, ἡ, *a generation*
γένεσις, -εως, ἡ, *birth, origin*
γένημα, -ατος, τό, *fruit, produce*
γεννάω, *I beget*

root ΓΝΟ, 'know'

γινώσκω, *I know*
ἀναγινώσκω, (*I know again*), *I read*

ἐπιγινώσκω, *I come to know, recognize*
γνῶσις, -εως, ἡ, *wisdom*
ἐπίγνωσις, -εως, ἡ, *knowledge*
προγινώσκω, *I know beforehand, foreknow*
γνωρίζω, *I make known*
γνωστός, -ή, -όν, *known*; as a noun, *an acquaintance*
γνώμη, -ης, ἡ, *opinion, counsel*
ἀγνοέω, *I do not know*

root ΓΡΑΦ, 'scratch, scrape' (signs in stone or wood)

γράφω, *I write*
γραφή, -ῆς, ἡ, *a writing, Scripture*
ἐπιγράφω, *I write upon, inscribe*
ἐπιγραφή, -ῆς, ἡ, *an inscription*
γράμμα, -ατος, τό, *a letter* (of the alphabet), *writing*
γραμματεύς, -έως, ὁ, *a scribe*

root ΔΕ, 'bind'

δέω, *I bind*
δέσμιος, -ου, ὁ, *a prisoner*
δεσμός, -οῦ, ὁ, *a fetter, bond*
ὑπόδημα, -ατος, τό (*that which is bound under* [the foot]), *a sandal, shoe*

root ΔΕΙΚ, 'show, point'

δείκνυμι and δεικνύω, *I show*
ἐνδείκνυμαι, *I show*
ἐπιδείκνυμι, *I show, prove*
ὑποδείκνυμι, *I show, indicate, warn*
ὑπόδειγμα, -ατος, τό, *an example, copy*

root ΔΕΚ, 'take'

δέχομαι, *I take, receive*
ἀποδέχομαι, *I accept from, receive, welcome*
ἐκδέχομαι, *I expect, wait for*
ἀπεκδέχομαι, *I wait for eagerly*
παραδέχομαι, *I accept, receive*
προσδέχομαι, *I receive, wait for*
εὐπρόσδεκτος, -ον, *well-received, acceptable*

προσδοκάω, I wait for
δεξιός, -ά, -όν, [δεκ+σ = δεξ], right (perhaps because the right hand is oftenest used in taking)

διάκονος, -ου, ὁ and ἡ, a servant, deacon, deaconess
διακονέω, I serve, wait upon, care for one's needs, minister
διακονία, -ας, ἡ, the office and work of a διάκονος, service, ministry

---

διδάσκω, I teach
διδάσκαλος, -ου, ὁ, a teacher
διδασκαλία, -ας, ἡ, teaching
διδαχή, -ῆς, ἡ, teaching

root ΔΙΚ, 'show, point'

δίκαιος, -α, -ον, righteous (in accord with the way pointed out)
δικαιόω, I justify, pronounce righteous
δικαιοσύνη, -ης, ἡ, righteousness
δικαίωμα, -ατος, τό, regulation, righteous deed
δικαίως, justly, uprightly
ἐκδικέω, I avenge
ἀδικέω, I wrong, do wrong
ἄδικος, -ον, unjust
ἀδικία, -ας, ἡ, unrighteousness
ἀντίδικος, -ου, ὁ, an opponent in a suit at law, an adversary
ἐκδίκησις, -εως, ἡ, vengeance, punishment

root ΔΟ, 'give'

δίδωμι, I give
ἀποδίδωμι, I give back, pay; middle, I sell
ἀνταποδίδωμι, I give back (in return)
ἐπιδίδωμι, I give to
μεταδίδωμι, I share with, impart
παραδίδωμι, I hand over, betray
παράδοσις, -εως, ἡ, a tradition (that which has been handed over)
δωρεά, -ᾶς, ἡ, a gift
δωρεάν, (accusative of the noun, used adverbially: as a gift, gift-wise), freely
δῶρον, -ου, τό, a gift

54

root *ΔOK*, 'beseem, befit'

δοκέω, *I think; I seem*
εὐδοκέω, *I think it good, am well pleased with*
εὐδοκία, -ας, ἡ, *good will, favor, pleasure, approval*
συνευδοκέω, *I entirely approve of, agree with*
δόξα, -ης, ἡ, *glory*
δοξάζω, *I glorify*
δοκιμάζω, *I prove, approve*
ἀποδοκιμάζω, *I reject (after testing)*
δοκιμή, -ῆς, ἡ, *a proving, approval, character*
δόκιμος, -ον, *tested, approved*
ἀδόκιμος, -ον *(failing to pass the test), unapproved, counterfeit*
δόγμα, -ατος, τό, *a (public) decree*

δοῦλος, -ου, ὁ, *a slave*
σύνδουλος, -ου, ὁ, *a fellow slave*
δουλεία, -ας, ἡ, *slavery*
δουλεύω, *I serve*
δουλόω, *I enslave*

δύναμαι, *I am powerful, able*
ἐνδυναμόω, *I endue with power, make strong*
δύνατος, -η, -ον, *powerful, possible*
ἀδύνατος, -ον, *impossible*
δύναμις, -εως, ἡ, *power*

ἔλεος, -ους, τό, *pity, mercy*
ἐλεέω, *I have mercy*
ἐλεημοσύνη, -ης, ἡ, *alms*

root *'EPX*, 'come, go'

ἔρχομαι, *I come, go*
ἀπέρχομαι, *I depart*
διέρχομαι, *I pass through*
εἰσέρχομαι, *I go in*
ἐξέρχομαι, *I go out*
ἐπέρχομαι, *I come upon* (sometimes with hostility)
κατέρχομαι, *I come down, go down*

παρέρχομαι, *I pass by, pass away*
προέρχομαι, *I go before*
προσέρχομαι, *I come to*
συνέρχομαι, *I come together*

root 'ΕΣ, 'be'

εἰμί, *I am*
ἄπειμι, *I am absent*
πάρειμι, *I am present*; *I have arrived*
παρουσία, -ας, ἡ, *presence, coming* (especially Christ's [second] coming in glory)
ἔξεστι, *it is permitted, it is lawful*
ἐξουσία, -ας, ἡ, *authority*

root 'ΕΧ and ΣΕΧ, 'have'

ἔχω, *I have, hold*
ἀνέχομαι, (*I bear up*), *I endure*
ἀνεκτός, -όν, *bearable, tolerable*
ἀπέχω, *I have received* (payment); *I am distant*
ἐπέχω, *I hold out, give attention to*
κατέχω, *I hold fast, hold back*
μετέχω, *I have a share in, partake of*
μέτοχος, -ον, *sharing in*; as a noun, *a partner*
παρέχω, *I offer, afford*
προσέχω, *I attend to, give heed to*
συνέχω, (*I hold together, constrain*), *I hold fast, oppress*
ὑπερέχω, (*I hold over, above*), *I rise above, am superior*
ἔνοχος, -ον, (= ἐνερχόμενος, *held in, bound by*), *liable, guilty*
εὐσχήμων, -ον, *of elegant figure* (way of *holding* oneself), *grace, of good standing*
μετασχηματίζω, *I change the figure of, transfigure*

root ϜΕΡ, 'speak'

ἐρῶ, (from a rare present stem, εἴρω), *I shall say*
ῥῆμα, -ατος, τό, *a word*
παρρησία, -ας, ἡ, *boldness* (of speech), *confidence*
παρρησιάζομαι, *I speak boldly*

56

root ϜΕΡΓ, 'work'

ἔργον, -ου, τό, work
ἐργάτης, -ου, ὁ, a workman
ἐνεργέω, I work, effect
συνεργέω, I work along with, co-operate with
συνεργός, -οῦ, ὁ and ἡ, a fellow worker
ἐργάζομαι, I work
ἐργασία, -ας, ἡ, work, business, profit
κατεργάζομαι, I work out
γεωργός, -οῦ, ὁ, (a worker in the earth [γῆ]), a farmer
λειτουργός, -οῦ, ὁ, (a public [λαός] minister), a servant
πανουργία, -ας, ἡ, (ability to do anything, cleverness), craftiness, cunning
ἀργός, -όν, idle, lazy (contracted from ἀ-εργός)
καταργέω, I bring to naught, abolish

root ϜΙΔ, 'see'

εἶδον, I saw
εἶδος, -ους, τό, visible form, shape
εἴδωλον, -ου, τό, an image, idol
εἰδωλολάτρης, -ου, ὁ, an idolater
οἶδα, (second perfect [I have seen] with present sense), I know
ᾅδης, -ου, ὁ, (α privative and ϝιδ, the unseen world), Hades

ζάω, I live
ζωή, -ῆς, ἡ, life
ζῷον, -ου, τό, a living creature, an animal

ζητέω, I seek
ἐκζητέω, I seek out
ἐπιζητέω, I seek for
συνζητέω, I question with, discuss
ζήτημα, -ατος, τό, a question, debate
ζήτησις, -εως, ἡ, a questioning, debate

root ΘΑΝ, 'die'

θνήσκω, I die; perfect tense, I am dead
θνητός, -ή, -όν, liable to death, mortal

57

ἀποθνήσκω, *I die*
θάνατος, -ου, ὁ, *death*
θανατόω, *I put to death*

root ΘΕ, 'put, set, place'

τίθημι, *I place*
ἀποτίθεμαι, *I put off from myself, lay aside*
διατίθημι, *I appoint, make a covenant*
ἐπιτίθημι, *I lay upon*
μετατίθημι, *I transfer, change*
παρατίθημι, *I set before*; middle, *I entrust*
περιτίθημι, *I place around, clothe*
προστίθημι, *I add, I add to*
ἀθετέω, *I reject*
θεμέλιος, -ου, ὁ, *a foundation*
θεμελιόω, *I lay the foundation of, establish*
ἀποθήκη, -ης, ἡ, *a storehouse, granary, barn*
διαθήκη, -ης, ἡ, *a covenant*
ἀνάθεμα, -ατος, τό, (a thing laid by or set up; a thing devoted to the vengeance of God), *a curse, a man accursed*

root ΘΥ (1), 'burn, smoke'

θύω, *I sacrifice, kill*
θυμίαμα, -ατος, τό, *incense*
θυσία, -ας, ἡ, *a sacrifice*
θυσιαστήριον, -ου, τό, (*a place for sacrifice*), *an altar*

root ΘΥ (2), 'rush'

θυμός, -οῦ, ὁ, *wrath*
ἐπιθυμέω, (*I have it upon my heart*), *I desire*
ἐπιθυμία, -ας, ἡ, *eager desire, passion*
μακροθυμέω, *I am patient*
μακροθυμία, -ας, ἡ, *long-suffering*
ὁμοθυμαδόν, *with one accord*
προθυμία, -ας, ἡ, *eagerness, enthusiasm*

58

root ʽΙ, 'set in motion'

ἄνεσις, -εως, ἡ, a loosening; relief, rest
ἀφίημι, I let go, permit, forgive
ἄφεσις, -εως, ἡ, a sending away, remission
συνίημι, (I go along with), I understand
σύνεσις, -εως, ἡ, understanding
ἀσύνετος, -ον, without understanding, stupid

ἰσχύς, -ύος, ἡ, strength
ἰσχυρός, -ά, -όν, strong
ἰσχύω, I am strong

root ΚΑΘ, 'clean'

καθαρός, -ά, -όν, clean
καθαρίζω, I cleanse
καθαρισμός, -οῦ, ὁ, a cleansing, purification
ἀκαθαρσία, -ας, ἡ, uncleanness
ἀκάθαρτος, -ον, unclean

root ΚΑΛ, 'call'

καλέω, I call
κλητός, -ή, -όν, called
κλῆσις, -εως, ἡ, a (divine) call, invitation
ἐγκαλέω, I call to account, accuse
ἀνέγκλητος, -ον, not to be called to account, unreprovable, blameless
ἐκκλησία, -ας, ἡ, a church, the Church
ἐπικαλέομαι, I call, name; middle, I invoke, appeal to
παρακαλέω, (I call beside myself), I beseech, exhort, console
παράκλησις, -εως, ἡ, exhortation, consolation
παράκλητος, -ου, ὁ, an intercessor, helper, Paraclete
προσκαλέομαι, I summon
συνκαλέω, I call together, assemble

καυχάομαι, I boast
καύχημα, -ατος, τό, a boasting, a ground of boasting
καύχησις, -εως, ἡ, boasting

59

root *KEI*, 'lie outstretched'

κεῖμαι, *I lie*
ἀνάκειμαι, *I recline* (at meals)
ἀντίκειμαι, *I resist, oppose*
ἐπίκειμαι, *I lie upon, press upon, am urgent*
κατάκειμαι, *I lie down, lie sick; I recline* (at meals)
περίκειμαι, *I am compassed about with, have around me*
πρόκειμαι, *I am set before, am present*
συνανάκειμαι, *I recline together, feast together*
κοιμάομαι, (*I lie at rest*), *I sleep, fall asleep, die*
κώμη, -ης, ἡ, *a village*

κλῆρος, -ου, ὁ, *a lot, a portion*
κληρονόμος, -ου, ὁ, *an heir*
κληρονομέω, *I inherit*
κληρονομία, -ης, ἡ, *an inheritance*

κοινός, -ή, -όν, *common, unclean*
κοινόω, *I make common, defile*
κοινωνέω, *I have a share of, take part in*
κοινωνία, -ας, ἡ, *fellowship, collection*
κοινωνός, -οῦ, ὁ and ἡ, *a partner, sharer*

root *ΚΟΠ*, 'cut, strike'

κόπτω, *I cut*; middle, *I strike* (my breast or head in lamentation)
ἀποκόπτω, *I cut off, amputate*
ἐκκόπτω, *I cut out, cut off*
ἐνκόπτω, (*I cut into*), *I block, hinder*
προσκόπτω, *I strike against, stumble, stumble at*
πρόσκομμα, -ατος, τό, *a stumbling, a stumbling-block, an obstacle*
κόπος, -ου, ὁ, *trouble, labor*
εὔκοπος, -ον, *with easy labor, easy*
κοπιάω, *I toil*

root *ΚΡΑΤ* and *ΚΑΡΤ*, 'strong, hard'

κράτος, -ους, τό, *power, dominion*
κρατέω, *I grasp*
κρείσσων, (or κρείττων), -ονος, *better*

προσκαρτερέω, *I continue in* or *with*
παντοκράτωρ, -ορος, ὁ, *ruler of all, the Almighty*

root ΚΡΙ, 'separate'

κρίνω, *I judge, decide*
ἀνακρίνω, *I examine*
ἀποκρίνομαι, *I answer*
διακρίνω, *I discriminate*; middle, *I doubt*
κατακρίνω, *I condemn*
κρίμα, -ατος, τό, *judgment*
κρίσις, -εως, ἡ, *judgment*
κριτής, -οῦ, ὁ, *a judge*
ὑποκριτής, -οῦ, ὁ, *a hypocrite* (literally, *a pretender, an actor*)
ὑπόκρισις, -εως, ἡ, (*acting a part*), *hypocrisy*
ἀνυπόκριτος, -ον, *unfeigned, undisguised*

root ΛΑΒ, 'take, receive'

λαμβάνω, *I take, receive* (2nd aor. ἔ-λαβ-ον)
ἀναλαμβάνω, *I take up*
ἐπιλαμβάνω, *I take hold of*
καταλαμβάνω, *I undertake, apprehend*
μεταλαμβάνω, *I have a share of, partake of, get*
παραλαμβάνω, *I receive*
προσλαμβάνω, *I receive*
συλλαμβάνω, *I take, conceive*
ὑπολαμβάνω, *I take up* (by supporting beneath); *I welcome*; *I catch up*
  (in speech); *I suppose*

root ΛΑΘ, 'conceal'

λανθάνω, *I am hidden from, escape notice* (2nd aor. ἔ-λαθ-ον)
ἐπιλανθάνομαι, *I forget, neglect*
ἀληθής, -ές, *true* (not concealed)
ἀληθινός, -ή, -όν, *true*
ἀλήθεια, -ας, ἡ, *truth*
ἀληθῶς, *truly*

root ΛΕΓ (1), 'gather, pick'

διαλέγομαι, (*I pick out* [thoughts] *one from another*), *I dispute*
διάλεκτος, -ου, ἡ, *speech, language*
ἐκλέγομαι, *I pick out, choose*

61

ἐκλεκτός, -ή, -όν, chosen, elect
ἐκλογή, -ῆς, ἡ, a choosing out, election (in the New Testament always of
the divine choice)

root ΛΕΓ (2), 'say'

λέγω, I say, speak
λόγος, -ου, ὁ, a word, the Word
εὐλογέω, (I speak well of someone), I bless
εὐλογητός, -όν, blessed
εὐλογία, -ας, ἡ, a blessing
ἀπολογέομαι, I defend myself
ἀπολογία, -ας, ἡ, a defense (especially in a law court)
λογίζομαι, I account, reckon
διαλογίζομαι, I debate
διαλογισμός, -οῦ, ὁ, a reasoning, questioning

root ΛΥ, 'loose'

λύω, I loose
ἀπολύω, I release (loose from)
ἀπολύτρωσις, -εως, ἡ, (a releasing), redemption
ἐκλύομαι, I am unstrung, grow weary, become faint-hearted
καταλύω, (I dissolve), I destroy; I lodge (after having loosed the straps
and packs of the beasts of burden as well as one's own garments)
παραλύομαι, (I am unstrung), I am a paralytic
παραλυτικός, -ή, -όν, paralytic

root ΜΑ, 'reflex thought, persistency'

μένω, (I bethink myself, wait), I remain
διαμένω, I remain throughout
ἐπιμένω, I remain in
προσμένω, I remain with, continue in
ὑπομένω, I tarry; I endure
ὑπομονή, -ῆς, ἡ, patient, steadfast endurance
μιμητής, -οῦ, ὁ, an imitator
μιμνήσκομαι, I remember
ἀναμιμνήσκομαι, I call to remembrance
ὑπομιμνήσκω, I bring to remembrance
μνεία, -ας, ἡ, remembrance, mention

μνῆμα, -ατος, τό, (something that brings to remembrance), *a sepulcher, tomb, monument*
μνημεῖον, -ου, τό, *a sepulcher, tomb, monument*
μνημονεύω, *I remember*

root *MAP*, 'thoughtful'

μάρτυς, -υρος, ὁ and ἡ, *a witness*
μαρτυρέω, *I bear witness, testify*
μαρτυρία, -ας, ἡ, *testimony, evidence*
μαρτύριον, -ου, τό, *a testimony, witness, proof*
διαμαρτύρομαι, *I testify (solemnly)*

root *MEP*, 'part'

μέρος, -ους, τό, *a part*
μερίζω, *I divide* (make parts of)
διαμερίζω, *I divide, distribute*

root *NEM*, 'allot'

νόμος, -ου, ὁ, *a law, the Law*
ἀνομία, -ας, ἡ, (without law), *lawlessness*
νομίζω, *I suppose, think*
νομικός, -ή, -όν, *relating to law*; as a noun, *one learned in the (Mosaic) law, a lawyer*

root *NO*, 'know'

νοέω, *I understand*
νόημα, -ατος, τό, *a thought, a design*
διάνοια, -ας, ἡ, *the mind, understanding, a thought*
κατανοέω, *I observe*
μετανοέω, *I repent*
μετάνοια, -ας, ἡ, *repentance*
νοῦς, νοός, ὁ, *the mind*
νουθετέω, (I put in mind), *I admonish, warn, exhort*

οἶκος, -ου, ὁ, *a house*
οἰκοδεσπότης, -ου, ὁ, *a householder*
οἰκοδομέω, *I build, edify*
οἰκοδομή, -ῆς, ἡ, *a building; edification*
ἐποικοδομέω, *I build upon, build up*
οἰκονόμος, -ου, ὁ, *a steward*
οἰκέω, *I dwell, inhabit*
ἐνοικέω, *I dwell in*
κατοικέω, *I inhabit, dwell*
οἰκονομία, -ας, ἡ, *stewardship, arrangement, dispensation*
οἰκουμένη, -ης, ἡ, *the (inhabited) world*
οἰκία, -ας, ἡ, *a house*

root 'ΟΜ, 'like'

ὅμοιος, -α, -ον, *like*
ὁμοιόω, *I make like, liken*
ὁμοίωμα, -ατος, τό, *a likeness, image*
ὁμολογέω, *(I say the same thing), I confess, profess*
ἐξομολογέομαι, *I confess, profess*
ὁμολογία, -ας, ἡ, *a confession, profession*

root 'ΟΠ, 'see'

ὄψομαι, (ὄπ-σο-μαι), *I shall see*
ὀφθαλμός, -οῦ, ὁ, *an eye*
μέτωπον, -ου, τό, *forehead*
πρόσωπον, -ου, τό, *face*

πάσχω, *I suffer* (2nd aor. ἔ-παθ-ον)
πάθημα, -ατος, τό, *suffering*
πενθέω, *I mourn*

παῖς, παιδός, ὁ and ἡ, *a boy, girl, child, servant*
παιδεύω, *I teach, chastise*
παιδεία, -ας, ἡ, *discipline, chastisement*
παιδίον, -ου, τό, *an infant, child*
παιδίσκη, -ης, ἡ, *a maid-servant*
ἐμπαίζω, *I mock*

πᾶς, πᾶσα, πᾶν, every, all
ἅπας, -ασα, -αν, (used by some authors in preference to πᾶς after a consonant), all
πανταχοῦ, everywhere
πάντως, entirely, assuredly
παντοκράτωρ, -ορος, ὁ, ruler of all, the Almighty

root ΠΕΡ (1), 'press or drive through'

πορεύομαι, I go, proceed
διαπορεύομαι, I go through
εἰσπορεύομαι, I enter
ἐκπορεύομαι, I go out
παραπορεύομαι, I go past, pass by
ἔμπορος, -ου, ὁ, (one on a journey [especially for business]), a merchant
πέραν, beyond (on the further side)
διαπεράω, I cross over
ἀπορέω, (I lose the way), I am in doubt, perplexed

root ΠΕΡ (2), causal of ΠΕΡ (1), 'export for sale'

πιπράσκω, (for reduplicated πι-περ-ασκω), I sell
πορνεύω, I commit fornication; metaphorically of idolatry (in accord with Biblical imagery, the marriage relationshp between God and his people is broken by the worship of idols)
πορνεία, -ας, ἡ, fornication
πόρνη, -ης, ἡ, (one whose body is sold), a prostitute, harlot
πόρνος, -ου, ὁ, a fornicator

root ΠΕΤ, 'fly, fall'

πέτομαι, I fly
πετεινά, -ῶν, τά, birds
καταπέτασμα, -ατος, τό, a veil (spread out), a curtain
πίπτω, (for reduplicated πι-πετ-ω), I fall
ἀναπίπτω, I recline
ἐκπίπτω, I fall away
ἐμπίπτω, I fall into
ἐπιπίπτω, I fall upon
προσπίπτω, I fall towards, prostrate myself before

πτέρυξ, -υγος, ἡ, a wing
πτῶμα, -ατος, τό, (the fallen body of one dead), a corpse
παράπτωμα, -ατος, τό, (a fall beside), a sin, trespass

root ΠΙ and ΠΟ, 'drink'

πίνω, I drink
καταπίνω, I drink down, devour, swallow up
ποτήριον, -ου, τό, a cup
ποτίζω, I give drink to

root ΠΙΘ, 'bind'

πείθω, I persuade (bind myself)
ἀπειθέω, I disbelieve, disobey (not let myself be bound)
ἀπείθεια, -ας, ἡ, disobedience, rebellion
ἀπειθής, -ές, disobedient
πεποίθησις, -εως, ἡ, trust, confidence
πίστις, -εως, ἡ, faith, belief, trust
πιστός, -ή, -όν, faithful, believing
ἄπιστος, -ον, unbelieving, faithless
ἀπιστία, -ας, ἡ, unbelief
ὀλιγόπιστος, -ον, of little faith
πιστεύω, I have faith (in), believe
ἀπιστέω, I am unfaithful, disbelieve

root ΠΛΑ, 'fill'

πίμπλημι, I fill
ἐμπίπλημι and ἐμπιπλάω, I fill up
πλήρης, -ες, full
πληρόω, I fill, fulfill
ἀναπληρόω, I fill up
πλήρωμα, -ατος, τό, fullness
πλῆθος, -ους, τό, a multitude
πληθύνω, I multiply
πολύς, πολλή, πολύ, much; plural, many
πλείων, -ον, larger, more

πλεονάζω, I abound in, make to abound
πλεονεκτέω, (I have more), I gain the advantage of, defraud
πλεονεξία, -ας, ἡ, greedy desire to have more, covetousness

root ΣΑF, 'safe and sound, alive and well'

σῴζω, I save
διασῴζω, I save (rescue) though (some danger)
σωτήρ, -ῆρος, ὁ, a savior, rescuer, preserver, the Saviour
σωτηρία, -ας, ἡ, salvation
σωφρονέω, I am sober-minded, self-controlled

(σθένος, -ους, τό, strength, might [not in the New Testament])
ἀσθενής, -ες, weak
ἀσθενέω, I am weak
ἀσθένεια, -ας, ἡ, lack of strength, weakness, illness

root ΣΚΑ, 'cover, darken'

σκηνή, -ῆς, ἡ, a tent, tabernacle
σκηνόω, I dwell in a tent, encamp
σκιά, -ᾶς, ἡ, a shadow
ἐπισκιάζω, I overshadow, envelop
σκότος, -ους, τό, darkness
σκοτία, -ας, ἡ, darkness
σκοτίζομαι, I am covered with darkness, darkened

root ΣΤΑ, 'stand, set'

ἵστημι, I cause to stand; I stand
ἀνθίστημι, (I stand against), I resist
ἀνίστημι, I cause to rise; I arise
ἀφίστημι, I withdraw, depart
ἐνίστημι, I am at hand, am present
ἐξίστημι, (I set one out of his senses), I amaze, am amazed
ἐφίστημι, I stand over, come upon
ἐπιστάτης, -ου, ὁ, (one standing over another), a master (found only in Luke, used of Jesus)
ἐπίσταμαι, I understand, know
καθίστημι, I set, constitute
ἀποκαθίστημι and ἀποκαθιστάνω, I set up again, restore to its former state

67

μεθίστημι and μεθιστάνω, I transfer, remove
παρίστημι, I am present, stand by
προΐστημι, I stand in front, lead, rule, practice
συνίστημι and συνιστάνω, I recommend; I stand with, consist
στάσις, -εως, ἡ, a standing; an insurrection
ἀνάστασις, -εως, ἡ, (a standing up), resurrection
ἔκστασις, -εως, ἡ, (standing outside oneself), bewilderment, a trance
ὑπόστασις, -εως, ἡ, (a standing under), substance, confidence
ἀκαταστασία, -ας, ἡ, instability, disturbance, revolution

root ΣΤΑΥ or ΣΤΑϜ, lengthened form of ΣΤΑ

σταυρός, -οῦ, ὁ, a cross
σταυρόω, I crucify
συνσταυρόω, I crucify along with

root ΣΤΕΛ, 'set in order, equip'

ἀποστέλλω, I send away (with a commission)
ἀπόστολος, -ου, ὁ, an Apostle
διαστέλλομαι, I command, charge expressly
ἐξαποστέλλω, I send forth
ἐπιστολή, -ῆς, ἡ, (thing sent by a messenger), a letter
στολή, -ῆς, ἡ, (a piece of equipment, especially of clothes, apparel), a long
    robe, a festal robe

root ΣΤΡΕΦ, 'turn'

στρέφω, I turn
ἀναστρέφω, I return; I behave, live
ἀναστροφή, -ῆς, ἡ, conduct
διαστρέφω, I pervert
ἐπιστρέφω, I turn to, return
ὑποστρέφω, I return

root ΤΑΓ, 'arrange, order'

τάσσω, I arrange, appoint, order
ἀντιτάσσομαι, I range in battle against, resist
ἀποτάσσομαι, I separate myself, take leave of, forsake
διατάσσω, I command
ἐπιτάσσω, I command
ἐπιταγή, -ῆς, ἡ, a command, order, authority

ὑποτάσσω, I subject
τάξις, -εως, ἡ, an arrangement, order, right order, office

root ΤΕΛ, 'end'

τέλος, -ους, τό, end
τελέω, I finish, fulfill
ἐπιτελέω, I complete, perform
συντελέω, I finish, accomplish
συντέλεια, -ας, ἡ, completion, consummation
τέλειος, -α, -ον, complete, perfect, mature
τελειόω, I complete, make perfect
τελευτάω, (I come to the end of life), I die

τέσσαρες, -αρα, four
δεκατέσσαρες, -αρα, fourteen
τεσσαράκοντα, indeclinable, forty
τέταρτος, -η, -ον, fourth
τράπεζα, -ης, ἡ, (four-footed), a table

root ΤΙ, 'honor, pay'

τιμή, -ῆς, ἡ, honor, price
τιμάω, I honor
ἐπιτιμάω, I rebuke, warn
τίμιος, -α, -ον, honorable, precious
ἀτιμάζω, I dishonor, insult
ἀτιμία, -ας, ἡ, dishonor, disgrace
ἔντιμος, -ον, held in honor, precious, prized

τρεῖς, τρία, three
τριάκοντα, indeclinable, thirty
τρίτος, -η, -ον, third
τρίς, thrice, three times

ὑψηλός, -ή, -όν, high
ὕψιστος, -η, -ον, highest
ὕψος, -ους, τό, height, heaven
ὑψόω, I lift up, exalt

root ΦΑϜ, ΦΑ, and ΦΑΝ, 'shine, show'

φαίνω, *I shine, appear*

ἐπιφάνεια, -ας, ἡ, *an appearing, manifestation* (of Christ in glory)

ἀφανίζω, (*I make unseen*), *I destroy*; passive, *I vanish*

ἐμφανίζω, *I manifest*

φανερός, -ά, -όν, *manifest*

φανερόω, *I make manifest*

ὑπερήφανος, -ον, (*showing onself above others*), *haughty, disdainful*

φημί, (*I bring to light, make known*), *I say*

προφητεύω, *I prophesy*

προφητεία, -ας, ἡ, *a prophecy*

προφήτης, -ου, ὁ, *a prophet*

φωνή, -ῆς, ἡ, *a sound, voice*

φωνέω, *I call*

συμφωνέω, *I am in accord, agree with*

βλασφημέω, *I blaspheme*

βλασφημία, -ας, ἡ, *blasphemy*

πρόφασις, -εως, ἡ, *a pretense, pretext*

φῶς, (contracted from φάος), φωτός, τό, *light*

φωτεινός, -ή, -όν, *shining, brilliant*

φωτίζω, *I shed light on, enlighten*

root ΦΕΡ, 'bear'

φέρω, *I carry, bear, lead*

ἀποφέρω, *I carry off, bear away*

διαφέρω, (*I bear apart*), *I differ*

εἰσφέρω, *I bring in, into*

ἐκφέρω, *I carry out, bring out*

προσφέρω, *I bring to, offer*

προσφορά, -ᾶς, ἡ, *an offering, a sacrifice*

συμφέρω, *I bring together*; *it is profitable*

φορέω, *I bear, carry, wear*

καρποφορέω, *I bear fruit*

πληροφορέω, *I accomplish, satisfy fully, fully convince*

φορτίον, -ου, τό, *a burden, load*

root ΦΡΕΝ (in φρήν, *midriff, heart, mind*)

φρονέω, *I think*

καταφρονέω, *I despise, scorn*

σωφρονέω, *I am sober-minded, self-controlled*
ταπεινοφροσύνη, -ης, ἡ, *lowliness of mind, humility*
φρόνιμος, -η, -ον, *prudent*
ἄφρων, -ον, *foolish*
εὐφραίνω, *I gladden, cheer up; am glad, rejoice*

root ΦΥ, 'bring forth'

φυλή, -ῆς, ἡ, *a tribe*
φύλλον, -ου, τό, *a leaf*
φύσις, -εως, ἡ, *nature*
φυτεύω, *I plant*

root ΧΑΡ, 'rejoice'

χαίρω, *I rejoice* (2nd aor. pass. ἐ-χάρ-ην)
συγχαίρω, *I rejoice with*
χαρά, -ᾶς, ἡ, *joy, delight*
χάρις, -ιτος, ἡ, *grace, favor*
χάριν, (accusative of the noun χάρις used absolutely, *in favor of, for the pleasure of*), preposition with the gen., *on account of, for the sake of*
χαρίζομαι, *I give freely, forgive*
χάρισμα, -ατος, τό, *a gift* (freely and graciously given)
εὐχαριστέω, *I give thanks*
εὐχαριστία, -ας, ἡ, *thanksgiving*

χιλιάς, -άδος, ἡ, *a thousand*
χίλιοι, -αι, -α, *a thousand*
χιλίαρχος, -ου, ὁ, *a military tribune, captain*
τετρακισχίλιοι, -αι, -α, *four thousand*
πεντακισχίλιοι, -αι, -α, *five thousand*

χράομαι, *I use*
χρεία, -ας, ἡ, *a need*
χρηστός, -ή, -όν, (*useful, good*), *mild, comfortable, gracious*
χρηστότης, -ητος, ἡ, *goodness, kindness*
χρῄζω, *I have need of*
χρῆμα, -ατος, τό, (*whatever one uses, a thing*), *money*; plural, *riches*
χρηματίζω, (*I transact business*, hence, *consult, deliberate*), *I make answer*

71

(in an oracle), *I warn*; passive, *I am warned by God*; *I receive a name (from my business)*, *am called*

χρυσός, -οῦ, ὁ, *gold*
χρυσίον, -ου, τό, *gold*
χρύσεος, -α, -ον, contracted χρυσοῦς, -ῆ, -οῦν, *golden*

χώρα, -ας, ἡ, *a country*
χωρίον, -ου, τό, *a place, field*
χωρέω, *I make room, hold*
ἀναχωρέω, *I depart*
χωρίζω, *I separate, depart*

ψεύδομαι, *I lie*
ψευδομαρτυρέω, *I testify falsely, bear false witness*
ψευδοπροφήτης, -ου, ὁ, *a false prophet*
ψεῦδος, -ους, τό, *a lie*
ψεύστης, -ου, ὁ, *a liar*

APPENDIX I

THE INDO-EUROPEAN FAMILY
OF LANGUAGES

LANGUAGES, like individuals, are related to each other in families. According to two independent estimates, there have been 2,796 languages in the world and these may be classified into about 26 families.[1] The family of languages that is of most interest to the student of New Testament Greek is the Indo-European family. Besides Greek this family includes seven other sub-families of languages, the Indo-Iranian, Armenian, Albanian, Italic, Celtic, Germanic, and Balto-Slavic. (See Table I on pp. 74 f.)

What region was the common center, the home of the parent tongue from which all the Indo-European languages have developed, has long been a subject of discussion.[2] Earlier investigators were confident that it was in Asia—the continent which was the source of the oldest civilization, the traditional site of the Garden of Eden, and the locality where Sanskrit was spoken. But more recently certain scholars have favored the hypothesis that localizes what is popularly called 'the cradle of the Aryans' in the region extending north of the Black Sea and Caucasia, and south and west of the Volga River.[3]

Beginning about 3000 B.C. it is probable that successive migrations of tribes left the old home and drifted, some south-east to the Ganges valley, others westward throughout Europe.[4] No remains of the parent Indo-European tongue are extant, but, by means of comparative linguistics, scholars have been able to reconstruct a large part of its vocabulary and grammar.[5]

[1] Louis H. Gray, *Foundations of Language* (New York, 1939), pp. 417 f. and 303.
[2] The question has not yet been satisfactorily answered; for significant discussions see F. Specht, 'Sprachliches zur Urheimat der Indogermanen' in Kuhn's *Zeitschrift für vergleichende Sprachforschung*, lxvi (1939), pp. 1–74, and Giacomo Devoto, *Origini indeuropee* (Florence, [1962]).
[3] See, e.g., Harold H. Bender, *The Home of the Indo-Europeans* (Princeton, 1922), and Gray, op. cit., pp. 304–10.
[4] Today all of the languages of Europe belong to the Indo-European family except Basque, Esthonian, Finnish, Hungarian, Lapp, and Turkish.
[5] Works of this kind are A. Walde and J. Pokorny, *Etymologisches Wörterbuch der*

Table I. The Indo-European Languages

Extant modern languages are in the last column

Indo-Iranian	Indic	Vedic Sanskrit; Classical Sanskrit	Pāli, Prakrit dialects	Bengali Hindi Marathi Gujarati, etc.
	Iranian	Avestan Old Persian	Pahlavi Sogdian Sacian	Mod. Persian Kurdish Ossetan Afghan Baluchi, etc.
Armenian			Old Armenian	Armenian
Albanian				Albanian
Greek	East Greek	Attic-Ionic Arcadian-Cyprian Aeolic: Lesbian, Thessalian, Boeotian	The *koine* or Hellenistic Greek	Mod. Greek
	West Greek	NW Greek: Locrian, Phocian, Elean Doric: Laconian, Argolic, Corinthian, Cretan, etc.		(Tsaconian dialect)
Italic	Latin-Faliscan	Latin Faliscan	Vulgar Latin	French Provençal Catalan Spanish Portuguese Italian Rhaeto-Roman Rumanian
	Oscan-Umbrian	Oscan Umbrian Paelignian Volscian, etc.		

Table I, continued

CELTIC	Gaelic		Old Irish	Irish Scotch Gaelic Manx
	Britannic		Old Welsh Old Cornish Old Breton	Welsh Breton
	Continental	Celtic Inscriptions		
GERMANIC	East Germanic		Gothic	
	North Germanic		Old Norse	Swedish Danish Norwegian Icelandic
	West Germanic	Anglo-Frisian	Old English Old Frisian	English Frisian
		German { Low	Old Saxon Old Low Franconian	Dutch
		German { High	Old High German	German
BALTO-SLAVIC	Baltic		Old Lithuanian Old Lettic Old Prussian	Lithuanian Lettic
	Slavic	South Slavic	Old Church Slavic	Bulgarian Serbo-Croatian Slovenian
		West Slavic	Polabian	Bohemian Slovak Polish Wendish
		East Slavic		Great Russian White Russian Ukrainian

From Carl D. Buck, *Comparative Grammar of Greek and Latin* (Chicago, 1937), pp. 3f.

Several Anatolian languages of ancient Asia Minor (Hittite, Luwian, Palaic, Hieroglyphic Hittite, Lydian, Lycian) and Tocharian (A and B) of Central Asia also belong to the Indo-European family, but their exact relationships have not yet been fully determined.

75

The method and validity of comparative linguistics can be illustrated within one branch of the Indo-European family. The Romance languages are obviously related, for it can be observed that, within historic times, they have assumed their present forms in developing from their common source, the Latin language. Thus, for example, the Latin word *caballus*, meaning 'a pack-horse, a nag,' is the origin of Romance words for 'horse,' such as French *cheval*, Spanish *caballo*, Italian *cavallo*, Portuguese *cavalo*, Rumanian *cal*, Provençal and Catalan, *cavall*.[1] So, too, when the several sub-families of the extant Indo-European languages are compared, the hypothetical parent tongue may be reconstructed with a considerable degree of probability. Thus, the fact that the Greek word μήτηρ resembles the Sanskrit *mātár-*, Avestan (Old Persian) *mātā*, Old Armenian *mair*, Latin *māter*, Old High German *muoter* (modern German *Mutter*), Old Irish *māthir*, Old Slavic *mati*, etc., renders it highly probable that all these words have come from an Indo-European word **mātér-*.[2]

The words for 'horse' in the Romance languages, all of which have originated from the same Latin word, are said to be *cognate* to one another. So, too, besides words in English which are borrowed or derived from Greek (such as the derivatives supplied in Part I), other English words are said to be cognate to words in Greek. Cognate words, as their name indicates,[3] are words, in different languages, which are 'related' to each other because they have descended from the same ancestor. Although Greek and English have been separated from their common parent stock for so many centuries and have become widely different in so many respects, linguists have observed that some of the differences can be accounted for in terms of regular phonetic changes. Thus, because Greek and English are sister languages, it is possible to identify words in each which have descended from the same words in the primitive Indo-European speech. Jacob Grimm (1785–1863) formulated a statement of the mutation of consonants involved in the development

indogermanischen Sprachen, 3 vols. (Berlin and Leipzig, 1927–32), A. Meillet, *Introduction à l'étude comparative des langues indo-européennes*, 7th edn. (Paris, 1934), and H. Hirt, *Indogermanische Grammatik*, 7 vols. (Heidelberg, 1921–37).

[1] For still other dialectical forms, see W. Meyer-Lübke, *Romanisches etymologisches Wörterbuch*, 3rd edn. (Heidelberg, 1935), s.v. *caballus*.

[2] The asterisk signifies that this word does not appear in any historical source. For other derivations from this stem, see Walde–Pokorny, op. cit., s.v. *mātér-*.

[3] Latin *cognatus*, 'related (by blood).'

of the Teutonic languages.[1] (In all languages consonants are the skeleton-letters of words, for vowel-sounds are far from being as persistent—a fact which may be observed by noting the differing local pronunciations of the same words in our own language.)[2]

How Grimm's law operates is shown in the following table, which indicates what forms the consonants in the Greek group will assume in the English group, and illustrates them by a few examples. The Greek declensional terminations have, of course, no correspondence in the English words. Other words which might be thought to be exceptions to Grimm's law are accounted for by Grassmann's law and Verner's law.[3]

The consonants which are involved are those that form the so-called square of mutes:

	voiceless	voiced	aspirate
Labials (lip sounds)	π	β	φ
Dentals (teeth sounds)	τ	δ	θ
Palatals (palate sounds)	κ	γ	χ

1. The voiceless stops, π, τ, κ, are represented in cognate English words by *f*, *th*, *h*.

(a) π and *f*   *English cognate*

πατήρ 'father'   *f*ather

πληγή 'stroke, blow'   *f*lick, *f*log

πολύς, 'much'   *f*ull, *f*ill,

πούς 'foot'   *f*oot

πῦρ 'fire'   *f*ire

(b) τ and *th*

ὀδούς (stem ὀδόντ-) 'tooth'   too*th*

τρεῖς 'three'   *th*ree

(c) κ and *h*

καρδία 'heart'   *h*eart

καρπός 'fruit'   *h*arvest

κύων (stem κυν-) 'dog'   *h*ound

[1] For a most interesting account of the steps by which the present formulation of Grimm's law was attained, see Leonard Bloomfield's book entitled *Language* (New York, 1933), pp. 14 f. and 347-59.

[2] E.g. a man wears a 'doiby' hat in the Bronx, a 'darby' in Great Britain, and a 'derby' elsewhere.

[3] A succinct statement of these laws may be read in Webster's *New International Dictionary*.

77

2. The voiced stops, β, δ, γ, are represented in cognate English words by p, t, k.

(a) β and p   *English cognate*

βύρσα 'a hide'   *p*urse

κύβος 'loin'   hi*p*

(b) δ and t

δρῦς 'oak'   *t*ree

δύο 'two'   *t*wo

ὀδόντ- 'tooth'   *t*ooth

(c) γ and k

γένος 'race, family'   *k*in

γόνυ 'knee'   *k*nee

γινώσκω (stem γνω-) 'know'   *k*now

3. The aspirated stops, φ, θ, χ, are represented in cognate English words by b, d, g.

(a) φ and b   *English cognate*

φέρω 'I bear'   *b*ear

φράτηρ 'a member of a brother-

     hood'   *b*rother

(b) θ and d

θυγάτηρ 'daughter'   *d*aughter

θύρα 'door'   *d*oor

μέθυ 'wine'   mea*d*

τίθημι (stem θε-) 'I put, place'   *d*o

(c) χ and g

ὀχέω 'I uphold, carry, ride'   wei*g*h

χήν (dat. pl. χησί) 'goose'   *g*oose

χόρτος 'enclosure, grass'   *g*arden

APPENDIX II

PREPOSITIONS IN COMPOSITION WITH VERBS

ORIGINALLY a preposition was an auxiliary word which assisted in defining and clarifying the significance of the case of a noun.[1] When a preposition is compounded with a verb its primitive connotation may acquire various other functions and meanings. One of the most important of these is the so-called 'perfective' use of the preposition. When used in this way the preposition usually completes or emphasizes the action conveyed by the simple verb. All Indo-European languages employ prepositions in this perfectivizing sense. Compare, for example, the English verbs *bring* and *bring up*, *burn* and *burn up*, *carry* and *carry off*, *drink* and *drink up*, *eat* and *eat up*, *follow* and *follow up* or *follow through*, *go* and *go away*, *knock* and *knock down*, *make* and *make over*, *pluck* and *pluck out*, *speak* and *speak out*, *wake* and *wake up*, *work* and *work out*. In each instance the compound verb intensifies the sense of the simple verb. So too in Greek—although Greek and English do not always use the same preposition to convey the same idea. Compare ἐργάζομαι, *I work*, with κατεργάζομαι, *I work out* (literally *down to the finish*, see Phil. 2: 12); καίομαι, *I burn*, with κατακαίομαι, *I burn up, burn completely* (see Matt. 3:12); ἐσθίω, *I eat*, with κατεσθίω, *I eat up, devour* (see Luke 20: 47).[2]

In the following list each preposition is analyzed as to its principal meanings when in composition with verbs. Most of the semantic shifts are perfectly clear. Occasionally, however, the meaning of the compound verb cannot easily be determined from the separate meanings of its component parts. Thus, the force of ἀπό in ἀποκρίνομαι and in ἀποθνήσκω is no longer obvious. Perhaps originally the former verb meant 'I answer *back*' and the latter 'I die *off*'.

[1] See, further, A. T. Robertson, *A Grammar of the Greek New Testament in the Light of Historical Research*, 5th edn. (New York, 1931), pp. 553-7. The primary meanings of Greek prepositions used with various cases may be seen in Table II on p. 80.

[2] For additional information about perfective verbs see J. H. Moulton, *A Grammar of New Testament Greek*, vol. i, *Prolegomena*, 3rd edn. (Edinburgh, 1908), pp. 111–18.

TABLE II. GEOMETRIC ARRANGEMENT OF THE GREEK PREPOSITIONS

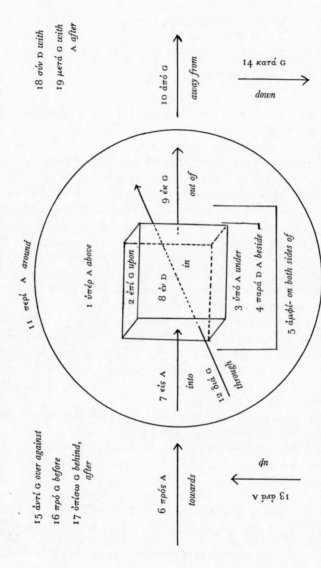

15 ἀντί G *over against*

16 πρό G *before*

17 ὀπίσω G *behind, after*

18 σύν D *with*

19 μετά G *with*
    A *after*

11 περί A *around*

1 ὑπέρ A *above*

10 ἀπό G
away from

14 κατά G

down

9 ἐκ G
out of

2 ἐπί G *upon*

8 ἐν D

in

3 ὑπό A *under*

4 παρά D A *beside*

5 ἀμφί- *on both sides of*

7 εἰς A

into

12 διά G

through

6 πρός A

towards

13 ἀνά A

up

Notes: 1. The symbols, G, D, and A should be read: 'with the genitive case means,' 'with the dative case means,' and 'with the accusative case means.' Number 5 appears in the New Testament only in compound words.

2. Only the basic meanings of prepositions with certain cases are given here. For other meanings with other cases, a lexicon should be consulted.

It will be remembered that a preposition which ends in a vowel drops that vowel when compounded with a verb which begins with a vowel, as ἀπέρχομαι from ἀπό and ἔρχομαι. The only exceptions to this rule are compounds with περί and πρό, which do not drop their final vowel, as προάγω and περιάγω.

ἀνά (1) Root meaning *upwards*
ἀναβαίνω, *I go up*
ἀνίστημι, *I cause to stand up*

(2) *Again, anew, thoroughly*
ἀναζάω, *I live again, revive*
ἀναπαύω, *I give rest to* (someone) *thoroughly, refresh*
ἀνασταυρόω, *I crucify afresh*

(3) *Back, backwards, to and fro*
ἀναστρέφω, *I turn upside down, turn back, walk to and fro, conduct myself, live*
ἀναστροφή, '*walk*,' *conduct*

ἀντί (1) Root meaning *opposite, against, over against*
ἀντιπαρέρχομαι, *I pass by* [παρά] *on the other side*
ἀντιλέγω, *I speak against, oppose, resist*
ἀντίχριστος, *an opponent of Christ, antichrist*

(2) *Requital*
ἀνταποδίδωμι, *I give back as an equivalent requital* (ἀντί expresses the idea of a full, complete return)
ἀντιμισθία, *reward, requital*

(3) *Substitution*
ἀνθύπατος (ἀντί and ὕπατος, an alternative form of ὑπέρτατος, *supreme*), *a proconsul*
Perhaps ἀντίχριστος should be classified here as 'one who assumes the guise of Christ'

ἀπό (1) Root meaning *away from*
ἀπέρχομαι, *I depart from*
ἀποκαλύπτω, *I withdraw a cover from, uncover, reveal*

(2) *Back again* (like Latin *re-*)
ἀποδίδωμι, *I give back, return*
ἀπολαμβάνω, *I take back, recover*

(3) *Perfective*

ἀπέχω, *I have fully, have received* (in full; see Matt. 6: 2, 5, 16); also in sense (1), *I am away, distant*; middle, *I hold myself off from, abstain*

ἀπόλλυμι, *I destroy utterly*; middle, *I perish completely*

ἀπολούομαι, *I wash myself thoroughly*

διά (1) Root meaning *through*

διέρχομαι, *I go through, pass through*

(2) *Distribution*

διαγγέλλω, *I publish abroad, proclaim*

διαδίδωμι, *I distribute*

(3) *Transition, change*

διαβάλλω, *I throw across, slander*

διαλλάσσω, *I change* (make other [ἄλλος] than), *reconcile*

(4) *Separation*

διασπάω, *I tear apart*

(5) *Perfective*

διαβεβαιόομαι, *I assert confidently, emphatically*

διακαθαρίζω, *I cleanse thoroughly*

διαφυλάσσω, *I guard carefully*

εἰς Root meaning *into*

εἰσέρχομαι, *I go into, enter*

ἐκ (1) Root meaning *from out of*

ἐκβάλλω, *I cast out*

ἐξέρχομαι, *I go out*

(2) *Perfective*

ἐκπληρόω, *I fill completely*

ἐξαπορέομαι, *I am utterly at a loss*

ἐν (1) Root meaning *in*

ἐνοικέω, *I dwell in*

(2) Motion *into*

ἐμβαίνω, *I step into* [a boat], *I embark*

82

ἐπί (1) Root meaning *on, upon*
ἐπιβάλλω, *I cast, lay,* or *put upon*
ἐπιτίθημι, *I lay, set,* or *place upon*

(2) Motion *towards*
ἐπέρχομαι, *I come upon* (sometimes with hostility)
ἐπιβάλλω, *I lay* or *put upon*

(3) *Upwards*
ἐπαίρω, *I lift up, raise*

(4) *Superintendence*
ἐπίσκοπος, *one who oversees, a bishop*
ἐπιστάτης, *one who is set over, a master*

κατά (1) Root meaning *down from, down*
καταβαίνω, *I go down*

(2) *Opposition*
κατακρίνω, *I give judgment against, condemn*
καταράομαι, *I pray against, curse*

(3) In succession, *in order*
καταρτίζω, *I set in order, mend*
κατευθύνω, *I make straight, guide, direct*

(4) *After, behind*
κατακολουθέω, *I follow after*
καταλείπω, *I leave behind, forsake*

(5) *Perfective*
κατεργάζομαι, *I work out thoroughly, accomplish*
κατεσθίω, *I eat up, devour*

μετά (1) Root meaning *association with*
μεταδίδωμι, *I share* (a thing) *with* (anyone), *impart*
μετέχω, *I partake of, share in*

(2) *Change, alteration*
μεταβαίνω, *I pass from one place to another, depart*
μεταμορφόω, *I change to another form, transform, transfigure*
μετανοέω, *I change my mind* or *purpose, repent*

(3) *After, in search of*
μεταπέμπω, *I send after* or *for, summon*

παρά (1) Root meaning *beside, near*
παραγίνομαι, *I am at hand, arrive*
παρακαλέω, *I call to my side, summon, admonish, entreat, encourage, comfort*

(2) *Violation, transgression, neglect*
παραβαίνω, *I go by the side of* (and beyond), *overstep, transgress*
παρακούω, *I hear amiss, hear without heeding, disobey*

περί (1) Root meaning *in a circuit about, around*
περιβάλλω, *I throw around, I clothe*
περιπατέω, *I walk about*, Hebraistically, in an ethical sense, *I conduct myself, live*

(2) *Beyond* (because that which surrounds a thing does not belong to the thing itself but is beyond it)
περισσεύω, *I exceed* (the ordinary, the necessary), *I abound, cause to abound*

πρό Root meaning *before* (of place or time), *forth*
προάγω, *I lead forth, go before*
προγινώσκω, *I know beforehand, foreknow*
προφητεύω, *I foretell, speak forth, prophesy*

πρός (1) Root meaning *to, towards*
προσέρχομαι, *I come to, approach*
προσέχω, *I bring to*; with τὸν νοῦν, *I turn my mind to, attend to, give heed to*
προσκυνέω, *I make obeisance to* one (in token of reverence), *fall down before, worship*

(2) *On, at*
προσκόπτω, *I strike* (the hand or foot) *against, stumble at*

σύν (1) Root meaning *together with*
συνάγω, *I gather together*
συνεργέω, *I work together*
συνίημι, (I bring together in my mind), *I understand*

(2) *Perfective*
συνθρύπτω, *I break in pieces, crush utterly*
συνκαλύπτω, *I veil (cover) completely*
συντηρέω, *I keep safe*

ὑπέρ Root meaning *over, above*

    ὑπερβάλλω, (*I throw over* or *beyond*), *I exceed, surpass*

    ὑπερέχω, (*I have* or *hold over*), *I am superior, excel*

    ὑπερνικάω, *I am more than a conqueror*

ὑπό Root meaning *under*, hence of subjection and compliance

    ὑποδέομαι, *I bind under* (the foot)

    ὑπομένω, (I remain under), *I remain, persevere, endure*

    ὑπάγω, (I lead under), *I withdraw myself, depart*

Appendix III. Table of Correlative Pronouns and Adverbs

	Demonstrative	Interrogative	Indefinite	Relative and/or Indefinite Relative
Simple	ὅδε, this (here) οὗτος, this (near) ἐκεῖνος, that (yonder)	τίς; who? which? what?	τις, someone, anyone	ὅς, who, which ὅστις, whoever, whichever
Place	αὐτοῦ, here, there ὧδε, hither, here ἐντεῦθεν, hence ἐκεῖθεν, thence ἐκεῖ, there ἐνθάδε, here, hither	ποῦ; where? πόθεν; whence?	πού, somewhere	οὗ, where, whither ὅπου, where, whither ὅθεν, whence
Manner	οὕτως, thus, so	πῶς; how?	πώς, at all, somehow, in any way	ὡς, as, about
Time	νῦν and νυνί, now τότε, then	πότε; when?	ποτέ, at some time, once, ever	ὅτε, when ὅταν, whenever, when
Quantity	τοσοῦτος, so great, so much	πόσος; how great? how much?		ὅσος, as great as, as much as
Quality	τοιοῦτος, of such a kind, such	ποῖος; of what sort? what?		οἷος, such as ὁποῖος, of what sort
Size	τηλικοῦτος, so large, so great	πηλίκος; how large? how great?		ἡλίκος, what size of

86

APPENDIX IV

PRINCIPAL PARTS OF SOME IMPORTANT VERBS

THE following list of principal parts is a summary of some of the important verbs in the New Testament. The seven irregular verbs which are given above on page 46 have not been repeated here. The enclosing of a principal part in parentheses signifies that no form of the tense system immediately derived from that part occurs in the New Testament. In some instances, however, compound verbs which involve that principal part are found in the New Testament. Because of the exigencies of space the definitions of these verbs have been severely limited.

PRESENT	FUTURE	AORIST	PERFECT ACTIVE	PERFECT MIDDLE	AORIST PASSIVE
ἀγαπάω *love*	ἀγαπήσω	ἠγάπησα	ἠγάπηκα	ἠγάπημαι	ἠγαπήθην
ἄγω *lead*	ἄξω	ἤγαγον, ἦξα	(ἦχα)	ἦγμαι	ἤχθην
αἴρω *take up, take away*	ἀρῶ	ἦρα	ἦρκα	ἦρμαι	ἤρθην
αἰτέω *ask for*	αἰτήσω	ᾔτησα	ᾔτηκα	(ᾔτημαι)	ᾐτήθην
ἀκούω *hear*	ἀκούσω	ἤκουσα	ἀκήκοα	(ἤκουσμαι)	ἠκούσθην
ἁμαρτάνω *sin*	ἁμαρτήσω	ἡμάρτησα ἥμαρτον	ἡμάρτηκα	(ἡμάρτημαι)	(ἡμαρτήθην)
ἀνοίγω *open*	ἀνοίξω	ἀνέῳξα ἤνοιξα ἠνέῳξα	ἀνέῳγα	ἀνέῳγμαι ἠνέῳγμαι ἤνοιγμαι	ἀνεῴχθην ἠνοίχθην ἠνεῴχθην
ἀπόλλυμι *destroy*	ἀπολέσω ἀπολῶ	ἀπώλεσα	ἀπόλωλα		
ἀποστέλλω *send* (with a commission)	ἀποστελῶ	ἀπέστειλα	ἀπέσταλκα	ἀπέσταλμαι	ἀπεστάλην
ἀφίημι *let go; forgive*	ἀφήσω	ἀφῆκα	ἀφεῖκα	ἀφεῖμαι	ἀφέθην
βάλλω *throw, put*	βαλῶ	ἔβαλον ἔβαλα	βέβληκα	βέβλημαι	ἐβλήθην

PRESENT	FUTURE	AORIST	PERFECT ACTIVE	PERFECT MIDDLE	AORIST PASSIVE
γεννάω beget	γεννήσω	ἐγέννησα	γεγέννηκα	γεγέννημαι	ἐγεννήθην
γίνομαι become	γενήσομαι	ἐγενόμην	γέγονα	γεγένημαι	ἐγενήθην
γινώσκω know	γνώσομαι	ἔγνων	ἔγνωκα	ἔγνωσμαι	ἐγνώσθην
γράφω write	γράψω	ἔγραψα	γέγραφα	γέγραμμαι	ἐγράφην
δείκνυμι show	δείξω	ἔδειξα	(δέδειχα)	δέδειγμαι	ἐδείχθην
δίδωμι give	δώσω	ἔδωκα	δέδωκα	δέδομαι	ἐδόθην
διώκω pursue, persecute	διώξω	ἐδίωξα	(δεδίωχα)	δεδίωγμαι	ἐδιώχθην
δοξάζω glorify	δοξάσω	ἐδόξασα	(δεδόξακα)	δεδόξασμαι	ἐδοξάσθην
ἐγείρω raise up	ἐγερῶ	ἤγειρα		ἐγήγερμαι	ἠγέρθην
ἐλέγχω convict, reprove	ἐλέγξω	ἤλεγξα			ἠλέγχθην
ἐλεέω pity	ἐλεήσω	ἠλέησα	(ἠλέηκα)	ἠλέημαι	ἠλεήθην
ἐλπίζω hope	ἐλπιῶ	ἤλπισα	ἤλπικα		
ἐρωτάω ask	ἐρωτήσω	ἠρώτησα	(ἠρώτηκα)	(ἠρώτημαι)	(ἠρωτήθην)
ἑτοιμάζω prepare	ἑτοιμάσω	ἡτοίμασα	ἡτοίμακα	ἡτοίμασμαι	ἡτοιμάσθην
εὐαγγελίζω preach the Gospel	(εὐαγγελίσω)	εὐηγγέλισα	(εὐηγγέλικα)	εὐηγγέλισμαι	εὐηγγελίσθην
εὐλογέω bless	εὐλογήσω	εὐλόγησα	εὐλόγηκα	εὐλόγημαι	εὐλογήθην
εὑρίσκω find	εὑρήσω	εὗρον	εὕρηκα	(εὕρημαι)	εὑρέθην
ἔχω have, hold	ἕξω	ἔσχον	ἔσχηκα		
ἥκω have come	ἥξω	ἧξα	ἧκα		
θαυμάζω marvel	θαυμάσ꙾μαι	ἐθαύμασα	(τεθαύμακα)		ἐθαυμάσθην
θεραπεύω heal	θεραπεύσω	ἐθεράπευσα	(τεθεράπευκα)	τεθεράπευμαι	ἐθεραπεύθην

88

PRESENT	FUTURE	AORIST	PERFECT ACTIVE	PERFECT MIDDLE	AORIST PASSIVE
θύω sacrifice		ἔθυσα		τέθυμαι	ἐτύθην
ἵστημι stand	στήσω	ἔστησα ἔστην	ἔστηκα	(ἔσταμαι)	ἐστάθην
καθαρίζω cleanse	καθαριῶ	ἐκαθάρισα		κεκαθάρισμαι	ἐκαθαρίσθην
καλέω call	καλέσω	ἐκάλεσα	κέκληκα	κέκλημαι	ἐκλήθην
κηρύσσω proclaim	κηρύξω	ἐκήρυξα	(κεκήρυχα)	(κεκήρυγμαι)	ἐκηρύχθην
κρίνω judge	κρινῶ	ἔκρινα	κέκρικα	κέκριμαι	ἐκρίθην
λαλέω speak	λαλήσω	ἐλάλησα	λελάληκα	λελάλημαι	ἐλαλήθην
λαμβάνω take, receive	λήμψομαι	ἔλαβον	εἴληφα	εἴλημμαι	ἐλήμφθην
λείπω leave	λείψω	ἔλιπον	(λέλοιπα)	λέλειμμαι	ἐλείφθην
λύω loose	λύσω	ἔλυσα	(λέλυκα)	λέλυμαι	ἐλύθην
μαρτυρέω bear witness	μαρτυρήσω	ἐμαρτύρησα	μεμαρτύρηκα	μεμαρτύρημαι	ἐμαρτυρήθην
μένω remain	μενῶ	ἔμεινα	μεμένηκα		
ξηραίνω dry up		ἐξήρανα		ἐξήραμμαι	ἐξηράνθην
οἰκοδομέω build, edify	οἰκοδομήσω	ᾠκοδόμησα		ᾠκοδόμημαι	ᾠκοδομήθην
πάσχω suffer	(πείσομαι)	ἔπαθον	πέπονθα		
πείθω persuade	πείσω	ἔπεισα	πέποιθα	πέπεισμαι	ἐπείσθην
πειράζω tempt	(πειράσω)	ἐπείρασα	(πεπείρακα)	πεπείρασμαι	ἐπειράσθην
πέμπω send	πέμψω	ἔπεμψα	(πέπομφα)	(πέπεμμαι)	ἐπέμφθην
πίνω drink	πίομαι	ἔπιον	πέπωκα	(πέπομαι)	(ἐπόθην)
πίπτω fall	πεσοῦμαι	ἔπεσον ἔπεσα	πέπτωκα		
πιστεύω believe	(πιστεύσω)	ἐπίστευσα	πεπίστευκα	πεπίστευμαι	ἐπιστεύθην

PRESENT	FUTURE	AORIST	PERFECT ACTIVE	PERFECT MIDDLE	AORIST PASSIVE
πληρόω fill, fulfill	πληρώσω	ἐπλήρωσα	πεπλήρωκα	πεπλήρωμαι	ἐπληρώθην
ποιέω do, make	ποιήσω	ἐποίησα	πεποίηκα	πεποίημαι	(ἐποιήθην)
πράσσω do, perform	πράξω	ἔπραξα	πέπραχα	πέπραγμαι	
σπείρω sow	(σπερῶ)	ἔσπειρα		ἔσπαρμαι	ἐσπάρην
σταυρόω crucify	σταυρώσω	ἐσταύρωσα	(ἐσταύρωκα)	ἐσταύρωμαι	ἐσταυρώθην
στηρίζω strengthen	στηρίξω στηρίσω	ἐστήριξα ἐστήρισα		ἐστήριγμαι	ἐστηρίχθην
στρέφω turn	(στρέψω)	ἔστρεψα		(ἔστραμμαι)	ἐστράφην
σῴζω save	σώσω	ἔσωσα	σέσωκα	σέσωσμαι σέσωμαι	ἐσώθην
τελέω finish, fulfill	(τελέσω)	ἐτέλεσα	τετέλεκα	τετέλεσμαι	ἐτελέσθην
τηρέω keep	τηρήσω	ἐτήρησα	τετήρηκα	τετήρημαι	ἐτηρήθην
τίθημι place, put	θήσω	ἔθηκα	τέθεικα	τέθειμαι	ἐτέθην
τιμάω value, honor	τιμήσω	ἐτίμησα	(τετίμηκα)	τετίμημαι	(ἐτιμήθην)
φανερόω make manifest	φανερώσω	ἐφανέρωσα	(πεφανέρωκα)	πεφανέρωμαι	ἐφανερώθην
φιλέω love	(φιλήσω)	ἐφίλησα	πεφίληκα	(πεφίλημαι)	(ἐφιλήθην)
χαίρω rejoice	χαρήσομαι				ἐχάρην

APPENDIX V

FEMININE NOUNS OF THE SECOND DECLENSION

THE beginner in Greek learns that, with a very few exceptions, nouns of the second declension ending in -ος are masculine in gender. The exceptions that occur most frequently in the New Testament are ἡ ὁδός and ἡ ἔρημος. Besides these two words, however, there are—surprisingly enough—thirty-three additional feminine nouns of the second declension in the New Testament, as well as eighteen other nouns of the second declension that are sometimes masculine and sometimes feminine. Examples of the second group include παρθένος and θεός; the former word, which is usually feminine, is masculine in Revelation 14:4, and the latter word is feminine in Acts 19:37, where it refers to the goddess Artemis (sometimes called Diana).

In several cases what now functions as a noun was originally an adjective of two terminations used with a feminine noun. In the course of time, however, the latter came to be omitted, and the adjective alone was felt to be sufficient. For example, the adjective ἄβυσσος, -ον, means *bottomless*; ἡ ἄβυσσος (supply χώρα, *place*) means *the bottomless place*, hence *the abyss*.

In the following lists the numeral which follows the definition indicates the number of times that the Greek noun appears in the New Testament.

A. *Feminine Nouns of the Second Declension*

ἄβυσσος, -ου, ἡ, *the abyss* (9)
ἀμέθυστος, -ου, ἡ, *an amethyst* (1)
ἄμμος, -ου, ἡ, *sand* (5)
ἄμπελος, -ου, ἡ, *a vine* (9)
βάσανος, -ου, ἡ, *pain, torment* (3)
βίβλος, -ου, ἡ, *a book* (10)
βύσσος, -ου, ἡ, *linen* (1)
διάλεκτος, -ου, ἡ, *a language* (6)
διέξοδος, -ου, ἡ, *a thoroughfare* (1)

δοκός, -οῦ, ἡ, a beam, a log (6)
εἴσοδος, -ου, ἡ, an entrance (5)
ἔξοδος, -ου, ἡ, a departure (3)
ἔρημος, -ου, ἡ, a desert, wilderness (as a substantive, 34)
καλλιέλαιος, -ου, ἡ, a cultivated olive tree (1)
κάμινος, -ου, ὁ, ἡ, a furnace (4)
κέδρος, -ου, ἡ, a cedar (1)
κιβωτός, -οῦ, ἡ, a box, ark (6)
νάρδος, -ου, ἡ, nard (2)
νῆσος, -ου, ἡ, an island (9)
νόσος, -ου, ἡ, a disease (11)
ὁδός, -οῦ, ἡ, a way, road, journey (101)
παράλιος, -ου, ἡ, a level place (1)
πάροδος, -ου, ἡ, a passing (1)
ῥάβδος, -ου, ἡ, a staff, rod (12)
'Ρόδος, -ου, ἡ, (the island of) Rhodes (1)
σάπφειρος, -ου, ἡ, a sapphire (1)
σορός, -οῦ, ἡ, a coffin (1)
σποδός, -οῦ, ἡ, ashes (3)
στάμνος, -ου, ἡ, a jar (1)
συκάμινος, -ου, ἡ, a sycamine tree (1)
τρίβος, -ου, ἡ, a path (3)
τροφός, -οῦ, ἡ, a nurse (1)
ὕσσωπος, -ου, ἡ, hyssop (2)
χαλκολίβανος, -ου, ἡ, burnished bronze (2)
ψῆφος, -ου, ἡ, a pebble, stone; a vote (3)

B. Nouns of the Second Declension, Sometimes Masculine, Sometimes Feminine

ἀλάβαστρος, -ου, ὁ, ἡ, (is also sometimes neuter), an alabaster jar (4)
ἄρκος, -ου, ὁ, ἡ, a bear (1)
ἄψινθος, -ου, ὁ, ἡ, wormwood (2)
βάτος, -ου, ὁ, ἡ, a thorn or bramble-bush (4)
βήρυλλος, -ου, ὁ, ἡ, beryl (1)
διάκονος, -ου, ὁ, ἡ, a servant, deacon (29)
θεός, -οῦ, ὁ, ἡ, God, a god, a goddess (1314)
θυρωρός, -οῦ, ὁ, ἡ, a doorkeeper, janitor (4)
κάμηλος, -ου, ὁ, ἡ, a camel (6)
ληνός, -οῦ, ἡ, rarely ὁ, a wine press (4)

λίβανος, -ου, ὁ, rarely ἡ, *frankincense* (2)
λιμός, -οῦ, ὁ, rarely ἡ, *hunger, famine* (12)
μάρμαρος, -ου, ὁ, ἡ, *marble* (1)
νεωκόρος, -ου, ὁ, ἡ, *a temple keeper* (1)
ὄνος, -ου, ὁ, ἡ, *an ass* (6)
παρθένος, -ου, ὁ, ἡ, *a virgin* (15)
σμάραγδος, -ου, ὁ, ἡ, *an emerald* (1)
συγκληρονόμος, -ου, ὁ, ἡ, *a fellow heir, joint heir* (4)

INDEX OF GREEK WORDS

The numerals refer to pages of the Frequency Word Lists

95

γένος 26
γεύομαι 30
γεωργός 27
γῆ 9
γίνομαι 7
γινώσκω 9
γλῶσσα 16
γνωρίζω 23
γνῶσις 22
γνωστός 31
γονεύς 26
γόνυ 35
γράμμα 32
γραμματεύς 15
γραφή 16
γράφω 10
γρηγορέω 24
γυμνός 31
γυνή 9

δαιμονίζομαι 33
δαιμόνιον 15
δάκρυ 36
δέ 7
δέησις 27
δεῖ 12
δεικνύω 20
δεῖπνον 29
δέκα 23
δένδρον 23
δεξιός 16
δέομαι 25
δέρω 31
δέσμιος 29
δεσμός 27
δεσπότης 39
δεῦτε 35
δεύτερος 18
δέχομαι 16
δέω 18
δηνάριον 29
διά 7
διάβολος 20
διαθήκη 20
διακονέω 20
διακονία 20
διάκονος 22
διακρίνω 27
διαλέγομαι 33
διαλογίζομαι 29
διαλογισμός 32
διαμαρτύρομαι 31

διαμερίζω 36
διάνοια 35
διατάσσω 29
διατρίβω 39
διαφέρω 33
διδασκαλία 26
διδάσκαλος 16
διδάσκω 13
διδαχή 21
δίδωμι 9
διέρχομαι 19
δίκαιος 14
δικαιοσύνη 13
δικαιόω 19
δικαίωμα 39
δίκτυον 35
διό 16
διότι 24
διψάω 29
διωγμός 39
διώκω 18
δοκέω 15
δοκιμάζω 25
δόλος 36
δόξα 10
δοξάζω 16
δουλεύω 23
δοῦλος 11
δράκων 33
δύναμαι 9
δύναμις 12
δυνατός 20
δύο 11
δώδεκα 14
δωρεά 36
δῶρον 27

ἐάν 9
ἑαυτοῦ 9
ἐάω 36
ἐγγίζω 18
ἐγγύς 21
ἐγείρω 11
ἐγκαταλείπω 39
ἐγώ 7
ἔθνος 10
ἔθος 35
εἰ 9
εἶδον 9
εἴδωλον 37
εἴκοσι 37
εἰκών 24

εἰμί 7
εἶπον 7
εἰρήνη 13
εἰς 8
εἷς 9
εἰσάγω 37
εἰσέρχομαι 10
εἰσπορεύομαι 27
εἶτα 33
ἐκ 8
ἕκαστος 14
ἑκατόν 29
ἑκατοντάρχης 26
ἐκβάλλω 14
ἐκεῖ 13
ἐκεῖθεν 23
ἐκεῖνος 9
ἐκκλησία 12
ἐκκόπτω 39
ἐκλέγομαι 26
ἐκλεκτός 24
ἐκπίπτω 39
ἐκπλήσσομαι 33
ἐκπορεύομαι 20
ἐκτείνω 30
ἐκτός 32
ἐκχέω 30
ἐκχύννομαι 37
ἐλαία 31
ἔλαιον 37
ἐλάχιστος 32
ἐλέγχω 28
ἐλεέω 21
ἐλεημοσύνη 33
ἔλεος 23
ἐλευθερία 37
ἐλεύθερός 25
ἐλπίζω 21
ἐλπίς 16
ἐμαυτοῦ 20
ἐμβαίνω 28
ἐμβλέπω 37
ἐμός 14
ἐμπαίζω 33
ἔμπροσθεν 17
ἐμφανίζω 39
ἐν 8
ἔνατος 39
ἐνδείκνυμαι 37
ἐνδύω 22
ἕνεκα 23
ἐνεργέω 26

ἐνιαυτός 32
ἔνοχος 39
ἐντέλλομαι 30
ἐντολή 15
ἐνώπιον 14
ἕξ 33
ἐξάγω 35
ἐξαποστέλλω 34
ἐξέρχομαι 9
ἔξεστι 21
ἐξίστημι 29
ἐξομολογέομαι 39
ἐξουθενέω 35
ἐξουσία 12
ἔξω 15
ἔξωθεν 34
ἑορτή 23
ἐπαγγελία 16
ἐπαγγέλλομαι 31
ἔπαινος 37
ἐπαίρω 27
ἐπαισχύνομαι 37
ἐπάνω 27
ἐπαύριον 29
ἐπεί 22
ἐπειδή 39
ἔπειτα 30
ἐπερωτάω 16
ἐπί 8
ἐπιβάλλω 27
ἐπίγνωσις 26
ἐπιγνώσκω 18
ἐπιδίδωμι 39
ἐπιζητέω 34
ἐπιθυμέω 30
ἐπιθυμία 19
ἐπικαλέω 21
ἐπιλαμβάνομαι 27
ἐπιμένω 29
ἐπιπίπτω 34
ἐπισκέπτομαι 37
ἐπίσταμαι 32
ἐπιστολή 24
ἐπιστρέφω 20
ἐπιτάσσω 39
ἐπιτελέω 39
ἐπιτίθημι 19
ἐπιτιμάω 21
ἐπιτρέπω 28
ἐπουράνιος 27
ἑπτά 14
ἐργάζομαι 19

96

ἐργάτης 30	θαυμάζω 18	κακία 37	κλῆρος 37
ἔργον 10	θεάομαι 25	κακός 17	κλῆσις 37
ἔρημος 17	θέλημα 15	κακῶς 30	κλητός 37
ἔρχομαι 8	θέλω 9	κάλαμος 35	κοιλία 25
ἐρῶ 13	θεμέλιος 30	καλέω 11	κοιμάομαι 28
ἐρωτάω 16	θεός 8	καλός 13	κοινός 32
ἐσθίω 10	θεραπεύω 18	καλῶς 20	κοινόω 32
ἔσχατος 16	θερίζω 26	καπνός 34	κοινωνία 27
ἔσωθεν 35	θερισμός 34	καρδία 10	κοινωνός 39
ἕτερος 13	θεωρέω 17	καρπός 15	κολλάομαι 35
ἔτι 14	θηρίον 18	κατά 8	κομίζω 35
ἑτοιμάζω 19	θησαυρός 29	καταβαίνω 14	κοπιάω 25
ἕτοιμος 29	θλίβω 39	καταβολή 37	κόπος 28
ἔτος 17	θλίψις 18	καταγγέλλω 28	κοσμέω 39
εὐαγγελίζω 16	θρίξ 31	καταισχύνω 34	κόσμος 10
εὐαγγέλιον 14	θρόνος 16	κατακαίω 34	κράβαττος 37
εὐδοκέω 26	θυγάτηρ 23	κατάκειμαι 35	κράζω 16
εὐθέως 20	θυμός 28	κατακρίνω 28	κρατέω 17
εὐθύς 16	θύρα 19	καταλαμβάνω 31	κράτος 35
εὐλογέω 18	θυσία 22	καταλείπω 24	κρείσσων 27
εὐλογία 30	θυσιαστήριον 25	καταλύω 29	κρίμα 22
εὑρίσκω 10	θύω 34	κατανοέω 32	κρίνω 12
εὐσέβεια 31		καταντάω 34	κρίσις 17
εὐφραίνω 32	ἰάομαι 23	καταργέω 23	κριτής 27
εὐχαριστέω 19	ἰδέ 22	καταρτίζω 34	κρυπτός 28
εὐχαριστία 31	ἴδιος 12	κατασκευάζω 37	κρύπτω 26
ἐφίστημι 26	ἱερεύς 21	κατεργάζομαι 25	κτίζω 31
ἐχθρός 21	ἱερόν 14	κατέρχομαι 30	κτίσις 27
ἔχω 8	ἱκανός 19	κατεσθίω 31	κύριος 8
ἕως 11	ἱμάτιον 15	κατέχω 28	κωλύω 25
	ἵνα 8	κατηγορέω 24	κώμη 23
ζάω 11	ἵππος 29	κατοικέω 18	κωφός 32
ζῆλος 30	ἵστημι 10	κάτω 37	
ζηλόω 37	ἰσχυρός 22	καυχάομαι 21	λαλέω 9
ζητέω 12	ἰσχύς 39	καύχημα 37	λαμβάνω 9
ζύμη 34	ἰσχύω 22	καύχησις 37	λαός 11
ζωή 11	ἰχθύς 26	κεῖμαι 24	λατρεύω 26
ζῷον 25		κελεύω 23	λέγω 8
ζῳοποιέω 37	καθάπερ 29	κενός 28	λευκός 25
	καθαρίζω 21	κέρας 37	λῃστής 31
ἤ 9	καθαρός 23	κερδαίνω 29	λίαν 35
ἡγεμών 27	καθεύδω 25	κεφαλή 14	λίθος 17
ἡγέομαι 22	κάθημαι 14	κηρύσσω 15	λίμνη 37
ἤδη 16	καθίζω 17	κλάδος 37	λιμός 35
ἥκω 23	καθίστημι 25	κλαίω 19	λογίζομαι 19
ἥλιος 21	καθώς 10	κλάω 31	λόγος 9
ἡμέρα 9	καί 8	κλείω 30	λοιπός 16
	καινός 19	κλέπτης 30	λυπέω 23
θάλασσα 13	καιρός 14	κλέπτω 34	λύπη 31
θάνατος 12	καίω 35	κληρονομέω 28	λυχνία 35
θανατόω 37	κἀκεῖ 35	κληρονομία 32	λύχνος 32
θάπτω 37	κἀκεῖθεν 39	κληρονόμος 31	λύω 18

μαθητής 9
μακάριος 17
μακράν 39
μακρόθεν 32
μακροθυμέω 39
μακροθυμία 32
μάλιστα 35
μᾶλλον 14
μανθάνω 23
μαρτυρέω 14
μαρτυρία 20
μαρτύριον 26
μάρτυς 20
μάχαιρα 22
μέγας 10
μέλει 39
μέλλω 12
μέλος 21
μέν 10
μένω 12
μερίζω 32
μεριμνάω 27
μέρος 18
μέσος 16
μετά 9
μεταβαίνω 37
μετανοέω 20
μετάνοια 25
μέτρον 32
μέχρι 27
μή 8
μηδέ 17
μηδείς 14
μηκέτι 25
μήν 28
μήποτε 23
μήτε 21
μήτηρ 14
μήτι 28
μικρός 17
μιμνήσκομαι 25
μισέω 19
μισθός 22
μνῆμα 39
μνημεῖον 19
μνημονεύω 26
μοιχεύω 31
μόνος 17
μύρον 32
μυστήριον 22
μωρός 32

ναί 21
ναός 18
νεανίσκος 37
νεκρός 10
νέος 25
νεφέλη 24
νήπιος 31
νηστεύω 27
νικάω 23
νίπτω 29
νοέω 33
νομίζω 31
νομικός 39
νόμος 10
νόσος 37
νοῦς 24
νυμφίος 29
νῦν 11
νυνί 25
νύξ 15

ξενίζω 39
ξένος 32
ξηραίνω 31
ξύλον 26

ὁ, ἡ, τό 8
ὅδε 40
ὁδός 12
ὀδούς 35
ὅθεν 31
οἶδα 9
οἰκία 13
οἰκοδεσπότης 35
οἰκοδομέω 19
οἰκοδομή 28
οἰκονόμος 40
οἶκος 12
οἰκουμένη 31
οἶνος 21
οἷος 32
ὀλίγος 19
ὅλος 12
ὀμνύω 23
ὁμοθυμαδόν 37
ὅμοιος 18
ὁμοιόω 31
ὁμοίως 21
ὁμολογέω 24
ὀνειδίζω 37
ὄνομα 9
ὀνομάζω 40

ὄντως 40
ὀπίσω 20
ὅπου 14
ὅπως 17
ὅραμα 35
ὁράω 12
ὀργή 20
ὅρια 35
ὅρκος 40
ὅρος 15
ὅς, ἥ, ὅ 8
ὅσος 12
ὅστις 10
ὅταν 11
ὅτε 12
ὅτι 8
οὐ 8
οὐ 24
οὐαί 19
οὐδέ 11
οὐδείς 9
οὐδέποτε 30
οὐκέτι 17
οὖν 9
οὔπω 22
οὐρανός 9
οὕς 20
οὔτε 13
οὗτος 8
οὕτως 9
οὐχί 16
ὀφείλω 20
ὀφθαλμός 13
ὄφις 32
ὄχλος 10
ὀψία 32

πάθημα 30
παιδεύω 34
παιδίον 17
παιδίσκη 34
παῖς 24
παλαιός 27
πάλιν 11
παντοκράτωρ 40
πάντοτε 19
παρά 10
παραβολή 17
παραγγέλλω 21
παραγίνομαι 19
παράγω 37
παραδίδωμι 11

παράδοσις 34
παραιτέομαι 35
παρακαλέω 12
παράκλησις 22
παραλαμβάνω 17
παραλύτικος 37
παράπτωμα 26
παρατίθημι 27
παράχρημα 28
πάρειμι 30
παρεμβολή 37
παρέρχομαι 21
παρέχω 30
παρθένος 31
παρίστημι 19
παρουσία 24
παρρησία 21
πᾶς 8
πάσχα 22
πάσχω 19
πατάσσω 40
πατήρ 9
παύομαι 31
πείθω 17
πεινάω 25
πειράζω 20
πειρασμός 26
πέμπω 14
πενθέω 40
πέντε 20
περάν 25
περί 9
περιβάλλω 24
περιπατέω 13
περισσεύω 19
περισσός 25
περισσοτέρως 37
περιστερά 40
περιτέμνω 29
περιτομή 20
πετεινά 33
πέτρα 30
πηγή 37
πιάζω 35
πίμπλημι 24
πίνω 14
πίπτω 14
πιστεύω 9
πίστις 9
πιστός 15
πλανάω 19
πλάνη 40

98

πλατεῖα 40
πλείων 16
πλεονεξία 40
πληγή 25
πλῆθος 21
πληθύνω 35
πλήν 21
πλήρης 30
πληρόω 14
πλήρωμα 29
πλησίον 29
πλοῖον 15
πλούσιος 22
πλουτέω 35
πλοῦτος 25
πνεῦμα 10
πνευματικός 24
πόθεν 22
ποιέω 8
ποικίλος 40
ποιμαίνω 38
ποιμήν 28
ποῖος 21
πόλεμος 28
πόλις 11
πολλάκις 29
πολύς 10
πονηρός 14
πορεύομαι 11
πορνεία 24
πόρνη 35
πόρνος 40
πόσος 23
ποταμός 29
πότε 27
ποτέ 22
ποτήριον 21
ποτίζω 31
ποῦ 17
πούς 13
πρᾶγμα 38
πράσσω 19
πραΰτης 38
πρεσβύτερος 15
πρίν 34
πρό 17
προάγω 26
πρόβατον 19
προέρχομαι 40
πρόθεσις 36
προκαρτερέω 40
πρός 8

προσδέχομαι 33
προσδοκάω 30
προσέρχομαι 14
προσευχή 20
προσεύχομαι 14
προσέχω 24
προσκαλέομαι 22
προσκυνέω 16
προσλαμβάνω 36
προστίθημι 28
προσφέρω 17
πρόσωπον 14
πρότερος 38
προφητεία 27
προφητεύω 22
προφήτης 12
πρωΐ 36
πρῶτος 13
πτωχός 20
πύλη 40
πυλών 28
πυνθάνομαι 38
πῦρ 15
πωλέω 25
πῶλος 36
πῶς 12
πώς 34

ῥαββί 30
ῥάβδος 36
ῥῆμα 15
ῥίζα 30
ῥύομαι 29

σάββατον 15
σαλεύω 31
σάλπιγξ 38
σαλπίζω 36
σάρξ 12
σεαυτοῦ 18
σέβομαι 40
σεισμός 33
σημεῖον 15
σήμερον 18
σῖτος 33
σιωπάω 40
σκανδαλίζω 21
σκάνδαλον 31
σκεῦος 25
σκηνή 26
σκοτία 29
σκότος 21

σός 23
σοφία 17
σοφός 26
σπείρω 17
σπέρμα 18
σπλάγχνα 38
σπλαγχνίζομαι 36
σπουδάζω 38
σπουδή 36
σταυρός 23
σταυρόω 18
στέφανος 28
στήκω 36
στηρίζω 33
στόμα 15
στρατηγός 40
στρατιώτης 23
στρέφω 25
σύ 8
συγγενής 40
συζητέω 40
συκῆ 30
συλλαμβάνω 30
συμφέρω 31
σύν 12
συνάγω 15
συναγωγή 16
σύνδουλος 40
συνέδριον 25
συνείδησις 21
συνεργός 34
συνέρχομαι 21
συνέχω 36
συνίημι 23
συνίστημι 30
σφάζω 40
σφόδρα 38
σφραγίζω 31
σφραγίς 30
σχίζω 38
σῴζω 12
σῶμα 12
σωτήρ 24
σωτηρία 17

τάλαντον 33
ταπεινόω 33
ταράσσω 28
τάσσω 40
ταχέως 40
ταχύ 36
τε 11

τέκνον 13
τέλειος 27
τελειόω 25
τελευτάω 38
τελέω 22
τέλος 19
τελώνης 26
τέρας 30
τεσσαράκοντα 26
τέσσαρες 20
τέταρτος 40
τηρέω 15
τίθημι 13
τίκτω 28
τιμάω 26
τιμή 18
τίμιος 34
τις 8
τίς 8
τοιοῦτος 16
τολμάω 30
τόπος 13
τοσοῦτος 27
τότε 11
τράπεζα 31
τρεῖς 15
τρέχω 27
τριάκοντα 38
τρίς 36
τρίτος 17
τρόπος 34
τροφή 30
τυγχάνω 36
τύπος 31
τύπτω 34
τυφλός 17

ὑγιαίνω 36
ὑγιής 36
ὕδωρ 15
υἱός 10
ὑμέτερος 38
ὑπάγω 15
ὑπακοή 31
ὑπακούω 26
ὑπαντάω 38
ὑπάρχω 16
ὑπέρ 11
ὑπηρέτης 26
ὑπό 10
ὑπόδημα 40
ὑποκάτω 38

99

ὥσπερ ξένοι χαίρουσι πατρίδα βλέπειν,
οὕτως καὶ τοῖς κάμνουσι βιβλίου τέλος.